Color Your Life!

How to Design Your Home
—With Colors From Your Heart
and
COLOR BARS©
Color Matching System

2nd Edition

Elaine Ryan

TAYLOR PRODUCTIONS, LTD
NEW YORK, NY

Color Your Life: How to Design Your Home With Colors—From Your Heart and
COLOR BARS Color Matching System
Copyright © 2005 Elaine Ryan
Second Edition

Printed in the United States.
For information, address GRM Associates, Inc., 290 West End Avenue, New York, NY 10023.
Telephone 212-874-5964

ISBN: 0-929093-17-8

Cover and Book Design: The Printed Page, Phoenix, AZ, www.theprintedpage.com

You are about to discover that YOU
are your own best color expert.

So, Color Your Life!

How to Design Your Home—
With Colors From Your Heart

Contents

"Color speaks to us in a language all its own and when we hear it, we react to it with our hearts."
—Elaine Ryan

Chapter One
Whatever Happened to Color?

"Whatever happened to color?" I asked myself as I sat in a client's home not too long ago. My client, Brooke, is a handsome woman with definite taste and great style. When she called me for an appointment, I was excited by the possibilities of designing her home with its panoramic views of the desert and the mountains. But, as I sat in her living room and listened to her describe the room she envisioned, my excitement vanished.

"I want to use vanillas and créme de caramel and butterscotch and chocolate throughout the house," she explained, almost swooning at the thought of these tones.

"Brooke," I asked, hesitating to break through her reverie, "aren't you really talking about brown and beige?"

"Oh, no," she protested, "I'm not." She continued to describe her ideas. "And over here," she gestured toward a large area, "I see a luscious créme de caramel sofa."

"Créme de caramel?" I gulped. "Créme de caramel is beige."

As we continued to discuss her plans, I realized that Brooke was not going to budge. When she rolled the colors off her tongue, she tasted butterscotch enveloped in ribbons of cream. She did not equate "chocolate" with brown or "vanilla" with off-white. In her view, these delicious shades were tempting and luscious. There was no way she would agree that butterscotch by any other name is a shade of beige.

As with so many other sophisticated Americans, Brooke was sold on a neutral-color world. She'd been told that beige is "dramatic" and that off-white is "always right." When I asked her if she planned to add any other color to her home, she assured me she would. "I'll introduce color through our artwork," she said easily.

Hers was a familiar and, I must add, depressing response. Brooke honestly believes that color is fine as long as it's framed and hung on a wall. But sit on it?

That's another issue entirely. As I listened to her describe the rooms she envisioned, my perceptions for her home faded. Good-bye persimmon and all the brilliant hues of the desert. Hello beige.

Faced today with a preponderance of beige and off-white interiors, it's difficult to believe that beautiful, natural color was not always banished from homes. In terms of historical perspective, this neutral-color experience is a relatively recent phenomenon. The Victorians, for example, used intense color and varied patterns with abandon. No one worried in those days that rooms would look "busy" or that families would tire of certain colors. Prior to World War I, color was used spontaneously in home interiors in the western world. Color was fun and natural. No one feared it. Obviously, something happened; but what?

To trace the disappearance of color from our indoor world, understand that, while interior designers do not always like to admit this, they, too, are influenced by other professionals—principally by architects and fashion designers. Let's examine these influences separately.

Although it's been almost a century since Walter Gropius founded the Bauhaus school in 1919, interior design is still reeling from Gropius' search for purity. In fairness to the Bauhaus concept, its intent was not to purge color from our interiors. The theme of this school was to start from zero in a quest for purity and honesty. Consequently, bourgeois frills and froufrous were stripped from buildings in the search for pure forms. The Bauhaus belief was in spare, lean, sculpted spaces. But as the Bauhaus school gained acceptance, and form and space were deified by subsequent followers of this school, slowly—if not deliberately—color disappeared from the interiors of our environments. Ultimately, where the world from ancient times to the first quarter of the 20th century had seen beauty in a profusion of hues, the modern, Bauhaus-influenced world saw only confusion in vibrant colors.

Probably no one was more confused by this development than interior designers. They had the unhappy duty of interrupting the architect's "flow of space" by designing furnishings for these stark interiors. The obvious interior-design solution was to minimize interruptions by controlling color and even eliminating it wherever possible. Enter beige, off-white, and white—walls, floors, ceilings, window treatments, and furnishings!

Yet, try as people might to live happily in this new, almost-colorless world, a natural hunger for color persisted. Tom Wolfe, in *From Bauhaus to Our House*, writes about this hunger. He describes a world "driven to the edge of sensory deprivation." He writes of a post-Bauhaus society "desperate for coziness and color." I agree completely. Whenever I see a "vanilla" or "caramel" sofa buried under mounds of pillows of many colors, I'm reassured that color is both natural and needed. We do have a natural need for color, a yearning which even large canvases splashed with brilliant colors and hung on stark white walls cannot completely satisfy.

Think for a moment about how color seeps into our everyday language. We say that we "see red," are "green with envy," or we are "feeling blue." These associations of mood with color are no accidents of the English language. They are living proof that color is basic to our lives. As long as people are able to perceive the brilliant colors of the earth, color remains part of our thoughts, dreams, and vocabulary.

No color, not even white, escapes this associative process. For example, many Westerners associate white with cleanliness. We think of hospital white, crisp and antiseptic. This white is not a color to be trifled with. It is authoritative, efficient, businesslike, sanitary, and serious. Nowhere in this mental image is the soft "angel of mercy"—which is the reason why I believe that instead of crisp white, nurses should wear pink. Or perhaps you associate white with purity. After all, babies are christened in white gowns, children are confirmed in white, and white remains the contemporary traditional color for a bride.

Suppose, however, that you lived in another part of the world. Instead of cleanliness or purity, you might associate white with the coming of age. Some African tribes paint their pubescent boys white to symbolize their forthcoming semen. In these parts of Africa, white means life. But in areas of New Guinea, white is used to symbolize death. One New Guinean tribal custom dictates that women in mourning coat their bodies with white clay to symbolize their grief and oneness with the departed. In Japan, white is also linked with death. There, a bride may wear white not as a symbol of purity, but to symbolize her "death" to her family as she begins a new life with her husband.

Life and death. The two extremes of living. Both are tied to white. Even the ancient Egyptians, who recognized the magnetism of color, saw white as having special powers. The white foam of the flooding Nile symbolized the milk of abundance.

Yellow has an equally powerful and varied story to tell. Aztec Indians dressed their bodies in yellow in celebration of the sun. Buddhist monks wear yellow robes as a symbol of piety and humility. Jews were forced by the Nazis to wear yellow armbands as the ultimate sign of condemnation, corruption, and cowardice.

Scrubbing color from our interiors, then, was no easy job. However, after almost 100 years, generations of women have grown up feeling comfortable with a neutral color scheme. Grandmothers, mothers, and daughters all installed wall-to-wall beige carpeting, just as their neighbors did. These women bought off-white or maybe—more daringly—brown sofas, just as their friends did. They felt chic in their beige and off-white homes and offices because everywhere they looked, they saw this style repeated. Their taste was reinforced, their choices reaffirmed. Beige then bred more beige; off-white cloned more off-white. As the years wore on, we bought the package: Flow. Room flowed into room, usually with only minimal colorful interruptions.

Even in the most austere neutral-color periods, however, certain prescribed interruptions were sometimes allowed. During the thirties, for instance, along with the obligatory beige and pervasive off-white, apricots and greys remained in vogue. To understand why every decade has one or two "fashionable" colors to call its own, it's necessary to recognize the other force that influences interior design: the world of fashion. Interior colors are carefully culled from the palette of high fashion. Fashion introduces new colors; interior design reflects them.

Interior colors have always followed fashion, as this quick reference illustrates.

Major Colors in Fashion	Major Colors in Homes
1900–1913 — Edwardian Era White; pale green; cocoa; brown as accent; mauve; black.	White; pale green; mauve.
1914–1919 — World War I Cream; olive drab; khaki; greige (gray-beige); black; brown; "Alice Blue" (named after Alice Roosevelt Longworth).	Créme; olive drab; greige; "Alice Blue" (only in French-style bedrooms).
1920–1929 — Jazz Age "Ivory créme;" brown; orange; black; silver sheen in beads and sequins.	Ivory créme; silver; black.
1929–1938 — The Great Depression Ivory; apricot; grey; blush peach; rose, from light to deep; navy; brown; black.	Ivory; apricot; grey; peach; rose; black.
1939–1949 — World War II White; khaki; brown; navy; forest green; maroon.	Eggshell; maroon; green.
1950–1959 — Postwar Boom Pink; grey; navy; beige; yellow; turquoise; cocoa.	Avocado green; pink; all shades of beige and cocoa.
1960–1968 — Age of Unrest Beige; black; emerald green; Wedgwood blue.	Wedgwood blue; white; rust; green; all shades of beige.
1969–1979 — Age of Personal Exploration Hot pink; bright yellow; parrot green; beige; white; denim; blue; earth tones (rust, gold, brown).	Beige; white; earth tones (rust, gold, brown).
1980s — Yuppie Years of Prosperity Mauve; red; black; apricot; peach; denim; grey.	White; beige; pale apricot; grey; mauve; red; denim.
1990s — Last Decade of 20th Century Red; black; green; apricot; denim	White; beige; blue; brown; taupe.
2000 — New Millenium 21st Century White; denim; burgundy red; pink, yellow; black; greens ranging from pistachio to leafy green; indigo blue; coral.	Yellow; red; beige; greens; Wedgwood blue.

It's important to know the colors that fashion designers select are visible expressions of economic and social conditions of their world. Moved by the horror and anguish of war, designers turn to deeper, sober tones. Khaki, the color of the military, is always popular during wartime periods. In those years when optimism runs high, fashion designers celebrate prosperity by introducing bright, happy colors. In difficult economic periods, they express the mood of the times with darker colors.

Fashion has always understood the power of color to tell a story. And so do we. We use color in our clothing to make a statement about ourselves, to project an image we want others to accept. A man will wear a colorful pair of golfing pants on Saturday afternoon, topping it off with a brilliant-colored cotton shirt. But on Monday morning, this same man goes off to work in a sober, somber, three-piece navy pin-striped suit. His Saturday outfit tells his friends that he loves sporty and fun. His Monday clothing proclaims him reliable, conservative, and serious. We accept that wearing certain colors delivers a message about who we are, yet we've been slow to consider how surrounding ourselves with color in our homes can also make a statement about us. Why?

Because it's easier to change our pants than our wallpaper. However, cost and convenience are only part of the issue. During the last 65 years, interior design has been caught in a crossfire. While Bauhaus-inspired architects have spawned neutral-color environments, the fashion industry continues to create new colors and color combinations every season. On the one hand, interior designers are urged to strip color from interiors, yet at the same time they see color-hungry clients eagerly buying clothes in each season's newest shades and tones. Is it any wonder that we've become confused?

In case this hasn't been bewildering enough, we must also contend with color experts. Although these color consultants have been around for years, during the intensely introspective seventies, eighties, nineties, and up to the time I'm writing this chapter in the 21st century, this field experienced a resurgence of interest. Elaborate tests appeared, relating color preference to personality. And some evidence does support many claims about the physiological effects of color. Experiments show that when people are exposed to bright colors their respiration rate, blood pressure, and brain waves increase. However, when attempts are made to link personality traits to color preferences, the findings often contradict each other.

For instance, one well-known authority purports that people who prefer blue-green are over thirty-five and "probably divorced." Another insists that "uncomplicated people" like this color. A third expert notes that turquoise is preferred by people who are "experienced in life." No doubt this expert likes the color, for he adds that "this preference indicates a person of discrimination, clearly a person of good taste." And a fourth color consultant warns that a person who likes turquoise is "good looking but probably cannot get along with people."

According to these interpretations, if you like blue-green you are a terrific looking, if simple, thirty-five-year-old divorced person who cannot get along with people, but nevertheless has had many discriminating, tasteful experiences in life.

Is it any wonder then that people began to fear using color? How much easier to avoid judgements by ignoring colors altogether! How much simpler to choose beige and white—colors that are rarely tested and therefore have no negative meaning.

Forget the experts and listen to yourself! You know which colors you love. You only need to awaken your color memory.

❖ Can you remember the colors you loved as a child?

❖ Now think what colors you react strongly to today.

❖ Can you identify why you like or dislike those colors?

❖ Are there any colors that you associate with a particularly happy time in your life.

❖ Are there colors you know you have a strong aversion to?

As you think about this, see if you can identify the association you have with those colors. As you revive your color memory, you'll find that it's sharper than you suspected. Don't be surprised if you find that you love one tone of a particular color, yet dislike another tone of that same color. Your mind registers and separates an infinite array of color, storing your reaction to various tones of colors. This makes it possible for you to love the color rose, yet feel very uncomfortable when confronted with a deep maroon.

You've often heard color consultants describe colors as "cool" or "hot." Just for fun, take a moment to jot down your own response to this list of colors. Consider the color and quickly note whether you think it is a "cool" or a "hot" shade.

Red	*Green*
Purple	*Coral*
Yellow	*Beige*

Now imagine walking into a room decorated in blue and green—both traditionally "cool" colors. It is August, the temperature outside is ninety-five degrees, and the air conditioning is broken. Have you lost or found your cool?

Try mentally walking into a cantaloupe orange, lipstick red, and bright white room on that same steamy August day with the air conditioning working. Are you feeling cool or getting warm?

You can see how "hot" and "cold" theories evaporate when faced with the reality of living with color. The truth is that if you spent your summers at the shore gazing at the ocean, chances are that blue will always have a cool connotation for you. You may also react similarly to green if you spent long lazy summer days in the mountains staring at the greenery. It's the association—not the color—that elicits your response. Most colors can be hot or cold. If you think of cozy winter fires when you see orange, orange is "hot." However, if it is your favorite color of sherbet, orange will likely conjure up "cool."

By now you probably see why clients are often encouraged to simplify their use of color. Hot and cold, nervous and calm, exciting and dull. Rather than expose yourself to this confusing profusion of mixed color messages, you're told to stick to simple, soothing, always-safe beige.

Thank heavens Louis Comfort Tiffany never worried about mixed-color messages when he designed his marvelous stained glass windows and lampshades! Tiffany never heard the clashing of colors and used all colors freely because he knew that all colors are compatible with each other.

I remember vividly a raw, windy San Francisco day in 1981, as I stood in a line that stretched nearly around the block, waiting to get into the de Young Museum to see the Tiffany exhibition. People had driven miles for the privilege of experiencing Tiffany's brilliant world even for an hour. But it wasn't his technique they had come to marvel at; they were there to revel in his uninhibited color sense. They were there because color lights up every sense in our bodies and our minds.

History confirms that color is a natural element of life, and every culture has expressed itself in vivid, living color. Color, truly, is the language of living. When we deny ourselves access to color, as we have during certain periods of history, we deprive ourselves of one of our fundamental needs. We are meant to live in a loving relationship with color just as we are meant to live in loving relationships with our family and our friends.

Now that you understand why you fear using color in your home, you are ready for the supreme test: Facing your mother.

Chapter Two
You and Your Mother

Because your mother created your original home, she is the expert of all decorating experts, the Decorator's Decorator. Consequently, every woman, proud of her new home, naturally wants her mother to walk into it and say, "I love your home. I really do love it. It's so lovely."

Instead, this happens: You've spent nine months working with a professional designer who came highly recommended by all your friends. Everything is in place and you're ready for the grand unveiling. You telephone your mother, who lives out-of-state, and invite her to visit—to spend the two weeks you and she have talking about this past year with you and your husband and her grandchild.

Your mother is delighted to come. In the course of the conversation you tell her about your husband, about the business, about the baby. You do not tell her about the living room because you know you want to be right there in person when you see her initial reaction to your beautiful, newly decorated home. You can't wait to see her face when she walks through the front door.

At last the day dawns. You dust and vacuum. Fresh flowers are in your favorite crystal vase on the coffee table. You even wipe off the top of the picture frames just in case she checks.

You watch the clock anxiously. Finally she arrives. You throw open the front door to greet her and lead her into your newly carpeted and upholstered living room. Your pride and joy. She looks around. Then she turns to you and says, "It's nice."

It's nice? After all your anticipation of watching your mother see your home for the first time the only comment she has is "it's nice." To you "nice" sounds like the kiss of death.

You try to tell yourself that it doesn't matter that she didn't give you a rave review. You remind yourself that you always hated that awful blue sofa in her living room. But nothing works. All you hear is, "It's nice."

Worse yet, later that evening when you go over her reaction, reliving every difficult detail, you suddenly remember "the eyebrow." Your mother raised her right eyebrow a fraction of an inch as she uttered those awful words, "It's nice." Between the eyebrow and "it's nice," she had drained all the joy you were feeling about your new living room.

Every daughter knows that a mother's look says more than the Bible, the Magna Carta, or the Constitution of the United States. The mother gives "the look;" the daughter panics, thinking, "How can I please her?"

Our mother's approval and acceptance is something that all of us desire. Whether we are fifteen, thirty-five, or fifty-five, we always wonder about our mother's reaction. Our need to have our mother's approval has nothing to do with whether or not we like our mother's taste—or even our mother.

When I was growing up my mother lived by one motto: "Protect the Upholstery." Every piece of furniture in our living room was slip covered with plastic. I distinctly remember my mother's living room occasional chairs—an appropriate name for them because we used the living room only on special occasions. The chairs were upholstered in a lovely shade of turquoise, and the seats were so tightly sprung they looked like twin derby hats. We perched on those derbies for years and they never sagged. As were many other pieces of furniture in our home, these chairs were slip covered in clear plastic. This meant that, depending upon the season, we either stuck to them or we slid off of them.

As so many women of her generation did, my mother took covering seriously. My mother's "covering" practice has led to my forming some unusual color associations. For example, my brother and I never read the Friday paper sitting down. We always read it kneeling on the floor, on our hands and knees because Mother used it to cover the clean kitchen floor. First the floor was scrubbed; then she'd preserve it with the *New York Times*. It made for very interesting reading. Page three would be at the entrance to the living room and page four in the back hall. To this day, when I remember the color of our kitchen floor when I was growing up, I see black and white.

From baby bunting to wedding gown, your mother is your personal taste consultant. She conditions you to like or dislike colors and styles. When you're young, she dresses you. As you get older, she takes you shopping and guides your choices. And as you mature, you've become conditioned to seek her approval. She is the original Good Housekeeping Seal of Approval. Is it any wonder that you feel miserable when she looks at your newly decorated living room and says, "That's nice"?

In reality, your mother is only one of many people who condition you to color and styles. Conditioning is a constant process. When you look at a magazine and see photographs of a favorite celebrity's fabulous home, you're being conditioned to styles and colors. When you walk into a friend's home and respond positively to it, your conditioned reaction is taking place. It's natural to emulate people we admire. What child doesn't want to dress as her best friend dresses? Dressing alike is akin to an unspoken declaration of friendship, and in friendship we experience a delicious sense of security.

As adults we also want to feel accepted and want to please those we care about. And because our homes are extensions of ourselves, we equate approval of our homes with approval of ourselves. Yet, while approval is very necessary to us, our sense of independence is equally crucial. Consequently, while we strive to please others, at the same time we feel compelled to develop and protect our own sense of style and thus our own identity. At the same time, this is where we can run into problems.

Let's take a simple example. Beth grew up in a home filled with red and black authentic oriental furniture. Her mother adored lacquered everything. Throughout Beth's childhood her mother hinted that when Beth married, she could choose any of the bright red or shiny black pieces she wanted for her own home. For the first twenty-seven years of her life, Beth did not give the furniture much thought. Then she met Gregory.

A few months after the wedding, Beth's mother was ready to deliver. She called her daughter and told her that she was ready to make good on her promise. "Which pieces do you want?" she asked. Anything you want I'll have sent to you."

Beth begged off, saying that they were not settled yet. A year went by and Beth continued to think about the furniture. It looked right in her mother's home, but neither the bright red nor the shiny black was their taste. She and Gregory loved the light teak tones of Scandinavian furniture and by this time she was convinced that her mother would understand.

When Beth's mother came to visit, Beth and Gregory proudly showed off their apartment. Beth pointed with pride to their newest acquisition, a teak coffee table with a low sheen. She heard her mother sniff. "I would think that you would want something brighter here. This table is nice dear, but my red lacquer table in front of the sofa would add a dash of excitement to the room."

This exchange left Beth feeling threatened and guilty, and her mother feeling rejected. Beth felt that she had two choices: she could give in and accept red lacquer into her life, or she could refuse her mother's gift, and feel guilty. Neither is satisfactory. Beth needed to know that she had another option. She could learn to live without the approval of others—including her mother's—by acknowledging her own sense of style and thereby, maintaining her own personal identity.

Here's the lesson: It is possible and reasonable to believe that you can learn to design your home for yourself instead of for your mother or any other person's approval. Although on the surface this sounds elementary, it isn't. Many of us spend a lifetime denying our own taste and style in an effort to meet the expectations of those people who are important to us.

Meeting others' expectations is only one factor that inhibits the development of our personal sense of style. On the more practical side, we also have to deal with furniture-shopping anxiety.

From earliest childhood, we're conditioned to feel at home in apparel stores. We're conditioned to believe that shopping for clothing is necessary and if you give it some time and thought, you can be reasonably certain of bringing home appropriate clothes with a minimum of trouble and expense. However, this matter-of-fact attitude evaporates when the object is a sofa instead of a sweater, a skirt, a suit, or any article of apparel.

While you certainly don't want to make a mistake purchasing an article of clothes for your wardrobe, you really *can't afford to make a mistake* when purchasing furnishings for your home. For example, should you find that you've made a mistake when you bought a sweater you don't like you can always hide it in your closet, but can you hide a sofa in your closet? Of course not. And therefore, faced with the thought of purchasing furniture for our living rooms, investing a sizeable amount of money in a new sofa that we later realize we don't like, we become understandably concerned about making a mistake. Because we know that even a single mistake can be very expensive.

Unfortunately, when it comes to shopping for home furnishings, often we have no positive role model to emulate. Even mother is unsure about buying furniture. Ask her about fashion this season and she's confident. Talk about a new sofa for the living room or a new dining room rug, and she voices concern, anxiety, and indecision.

"Harry," she says, "Have you noticed that the arms of the sofa are worn out? I can't decide: Should we have it recovered or should we get a new sofa? I really don't know what to do. I'm thinking that tomorrow I'll start looking." All this from your mother, the lady who can slice through a crowd of sale shoppers, dive into a stack of blouses, and pull out the exact size and style she needs in forty-five seconds flat!

Indecision and negativism are built into home-furnishing discussions. We hear this as children, and as adults we act it out. Without ever intending to,

Mother hands down her negative attitudes to us concerning furnishings for the home. Consequently, even a self-assured woman who knows exactly what she wants in her home can have second thoughts when faced with shopping for home furnishings. And, if you're unsure about your own taste and style, it's nearly impossible to overcome these negative messages. What's more, should you make a choice that differs from one your mother would make, you could find that she registers your decision as a personal rejection.

Given all this to deal with, it's a wonder any of us feel confident about our own taste and style. Fortunately however, some people instinctively do. These are the people who naturally know which colors, fabrics, and fashions look best on them and are able to translate this color and style sense in their homes, and create their own personal environments. But more often than not, we meet someone like Desiree.

At five feet eight and 115 pounds, she embodies every woman's fantasy. During morning workout class, when everyone in the class sweats, Desiree "glows." She wears clothes in beautiful colors and always has a high-fashion look that's exciting and uniquely her own. So, when you're invited to her house you know that you'll be seeing Desiree and her color and style sense, translated from fashion to her living environment. But instead, you're confronted with an enigma. As she shows you from room to room, your amazement turns to disappointment. Her house is done in tones of beige, brown, and white. Nowhere among all the colorlessness and blandness, is a hint of the vibrant Desiree you know. You cannot connect the elegant person and her marvelous color sense with this house. Her house.

What happened?

More than likely Desiree is a product of her upbringing. Although she feels at home in boutiques and department stores, she has no idea where to begin when faced with decorating her home. Not wanting to do battle with the house, she retreats to the "neutral zone." She cannot go wrong with beige, she reasons. Because she's uncomfortable making choices for her home, she gladly turns those decisions over to a professional designer who assures her that together—Desiree and her interior designer—they'll select the "right look" for her home. Accustomed to coordinating her fashions, she's happy to be shown what "goes with what" in her home. And although she has a vague sense that it hasn't turned out exactly as she would have liked; that her home doesn't quite feel like, or reflect her own style, she can't put her finger on what is wrong.

Knowing what is wrong is no mystery. Many of us can empathize with Desiree because we don't know where to begin to discover our own taste and style for our home. Although putting colors together for a wardrobe comes naturally to Desiree, deciding on colors for her home is exceedingly difficult. But, it doesn't have to be so.

Color Your Life will show you how to begin, how to discover your own taste and style, and how to have your home show your own true colors.

How to Know What You Like and What You Need

Begin with the obvious. To know what you like and what you need to create your very own personal environment, begin by exposing yourself to beautiful rooms. It's a simple process that begins with buying yourself a minimum of five new home decorating magazines such as *House and Garden, House Beautiful, Better Homes and Gardens, Southern Living, Architectural Digest*—those magazines that picture beautiful rooms furnished in all styles and periods from 17th century European to 21st century Contemporary.

Look at the pictures in each of these magazines and if a room has a mood you relate to—if you like the look of the room—clip it out of the magazine. Don't give any thought as to specific furnishings: Whether or not you like or don't like the bedside lamps shown in the bedroom, the way the windows are treated in a room, or the arrangement of the furniture. The exact lamp and anything specific you might want for your own room are details we're not interested in now. At this time you're using these pictures to get a sense of what you like; that you will later translate to your own personal style for your home.

Place your clipped photographs in a folder marked "Rooms I Love." And keep the folder handy. As you continue collecting pictures, the folder will be filled with the colors, styles, and periods of furnishings that you can live with comfortably.

Should you find that you like many colors and styles of furnishings, that's good. Not to worry. Why limit yourself to one or two styles or colors? After all, you're a person who laughs and also cries, who enjoys spending your time alone, and also in the company of other people. You have more than one mood and appreciate more than one style—in fashion, foods, vacation destinations, etc.—so should your home be furnished in only one style? Of course not. Your home should reflect the person you are. The interested and varied person you are.

Important: Making notes on the pictures will be a reliable instant reference for you later, so that you'll know the colors and styles of rooms and furnishings you're drawn to.

Your Personal Reaction Journal

What are the colors you like in the pictures you have collected?

_____

_____

What are the styles you like?

_____

_____

Verify your selection. Should you remember a friend's home you admire, a home that you feel you could move into and live in comfortably, make a date to go back for a visit to refresh your memory. Write down your impressions of the house, the colors used, the style and period of furnishings, or any detail you especially are drawn to. Can you describe how you feel in that home? What mood does it project?

_____

_____

_____

_____

Compare your answers in the first two exercises. You will see that your choices are similar, verifying to yourself that you do know what you like. Knowing what you like is the first step toward developing your own color and style sense.

_____

_____

Check out your Closet Clues. Go into your bedroom and open your closet. Select your very favorite outfit. Try to do this without analyzing which one you look thinnest in or which one you get the most compliments wearing. What color is it? Notice the colors of the other clothes you are especially fond of. Add these colors to your notes.

_____

_____

Do the same for your husband's clothes. Remember that his business clothes may not necessarily reflect his true color preferences. He may have to dress in certain styles and colors for his work. Look at the colors in his casual clothes like his tennis shorts or golf pants. Knit polo shirts are good indicators of the colors he likes. Note those colors here.

_____

_____

Now for the fun of it, let's test your color Mother-memory. What colors do you think of as the colors of your childhood home?

Record these too.

_____

_____

What colors does your mother prefer?

_____

Do you think of any of these colors as yours?

_____

Can you remember the colors of your childhood bedroom?

_____

Did you select those colors or were they selected for you?

_____

When you think of your mother dressed up to go somewhere special, what colors do you "see" her in?

_____

What colors did your mother dress you in most frequently?

_____

Do you wear any of those colors today? Do you use any of them in your home?

_____

There are no right or wrong answers to this quiz. You may find that you're using many of the colors your mother liked in your childhood. That's fine. This is merely an opportunity for you to think about the colors you are now using in your home. Discovering how you've been conditioned to choose certain colors for your home is the first step toward opening yourself up to a world of other colorful possibilities.

Identify the colors you are living with today. To do this you need to take a quick color inventory of your home.

_____

_____

_____

After you've read these questions and answered each of them you will have your own *Personal Reaction Journal* that will instantly enable you to be on your personal color selection track. Your *Personal Reaction Journal* will enable you to take the guesswork out of making color decisions. As you review your answers to the questions you'll able to see what colors you are now using throughout your home and you'll be able to decide on the changes you want to make so that your home looks and feels supremely personal and lovely to you. Although this basic diary can be used for any room in your home, I'm including some individual questions for other rooms in your home.

Select a favorite room in your home: Write down the color you see the most of when you think of that room.

_____

What colors do you see as accent colors in this room?

_____

What message does this room give when someone is standing in the doorway, or is already in the room? Is it an inviting feeling—comfortable, friendly, sophisticated, cool, charming?

_____

_____

Now, ask friends what color they see as the major color in this room. You may be surprised to find out that each of you has different color perceptions.

_____

_____

Ask your friends what message they feel your room gives off.

_____

_____

Take a closer look at the colors you are actually using throughout your home. List the colors of the backgrounds of all your rooms. Backgrounds include your walls, (paints, wall coverings) floors, (carpeting, tile, wood), and window treatments (draperies, shutters, curtains). If your wall covering, carpets or draperies are patterned, the dominant color may be the background color, although in some patterns you may perceive two dominant colors. List these colors.

_____

_____

_____

_____

How many other colors are you using in your home: on upholstery, woodworking, picture-frame mats, throw pillows, bedspreads or area rugs? Note the colors you use most throughout your home. You may be surprised to find how few colors you are presently using. List these colors.

_____

_____

_____

Read through your color lists. Would you say that the colors you are using are *your favorite* colors? Are these the favorite colors of anyone close to you?

_____

Which rooms in your home do you believe most successfully convey the feeling you want to project?

_____

What are the colors in these rooms?

_____

Ask your husband and/or children what their favorite colors are—what colors they'd like to have in this room. This question will enable you to understand how sensitive you are to their color needs. You may not want to admit it but if you are "Mother," you could be continuing the color-conditioning process. Your own taste will almost always influence the interior design of your family environment. Now, you are the decorating expert, the "Decorator's Decorator."

When I work with a client I always try to encourage the entire family to become part of the interior design process so that the Mother Supreme cycle is interrupted. Too often, a woman will make all the decisions concerning her home without consulting her husband or children. If I were working with you and your family, I would begin by identifying everyone's needs. As you start to think about adding color to your home, answer these questions.

How many people are in your family?_____

What are the ages of the children?_____

What are the ages of the adults?_____

What are the special interests of your children_____

_____

What are the special interests of the adults?_____

_____

Do you know the favorite color or colors of each member of your family?
List the colors you think each person likes the best._____

_____

To avoid potential color conflict areas—places where everyone wants his or
her own true colors to show—consider the following:

In which rooms do family members gather?

_____

How much time do family members spend together after dinner?

_____

What do you do together after dinner?

_____

Is there a special room provided for this activity?

_____

What are the colors in this room?

_____

Who selected those colors?

_____

Is everyone comfortable with these colors? Ask your family to comment on how they feel about the color choice for this room. Are the colors too dark? Are they too pale? Are they anyone's favorite colors?

_____

_____

You may be surprised to find that, although you are very careful selecting colors for your living room, (the room where you entertain company), you haven't given the same kind of attention to the family room—the room that is used the most by your family.

When you decide to add color to this room, consider everyone's favorite colors before making your selection. It's very possible—even probable—that you'll come up with a list of four or five colors. This often happens. One way to use these colors in your room would be in a patterned fabric for a new sofa and lounge chair, or to recover or slipcover your existing furniture. This fabric could easily include everyone's colors and also work with the draperies and carpeting already in your room. I'll show you how to use many colors in a room later in this book.

Determine any special needs you envision for your home. Think about your hobbies, about recent acquisitions like a large-screen TV or a computer. Consider the fact that your pets occupy this room with you. Do you feel that you have adequate space to enjoy hobbies? Would you like to give these and your other activities more room in your home?

_____

As you begin keeping a *Personal Reaction Journal* you'll find that you're building new and excellent knowledge of yourself and your family. As you record the colors you're using in your home, the styles you like, the look you want to achieve, and some of your specific needs, you'll find that you're gaining deeper insight than you had before you began your *Personal Reaction Journal.* You'll feel sure that the colors you want to use, or those that you're presently using in your home are *your colors.* You'll feel sure of the style and periods you want your home to have.

As you read and use *Color Your Life* you'll continue to add more of your personal information to your *Personal Reaction Journal.* By having this knowledge at your fingertips, you'll find that you've become aware of the home furnishings you're considering buying, and that having this knowledge allows you to make choices for your home with deeper insight to your needs.

You'll know what you want, and you will be able to achieve the feeling in your home that reflects you and your family. You'll accomplish what each of us wants to achieve: A home that uniquely reflects our personal taste and style. And when you think of your home, your spirit will smile.

To Note What You Want to Remember

Chapter Three
The Supermarket Test

You're ready to say good-bye to an all-beige world, but something won't let you do it. That "something" more than likely is too many years of hearing that you'll grow tired of a particular color, or that certain colors when used together "look busy." Magazines have shown you the beige-and-white way for so many years that you don't feel completely comfortable taking the plunge. After all, it's one thing to be told to throw away your inhibitions, but it's quite another to actually do it.

Or, you may have decided that you want a professional designer to rescue you by showing you all the colors that are "absolutely perfect for you". Many experts will be happy, for a fee of course, to show you which colors are right for you. Any one, or even all of these may be good solutions for you. But there is an easier way—The Supermarket Test—a method I developed where you'll discover the colors you'll be happiest living with—now and always—*your colors!*

The Supermarket Test springs from my own love of food. If I'm unhappy, a trip to the supermarket cheers me up. Where other women will turn to jewelry, I'll pick up a pineapple. I find that the gorgeous colors of fruits and vegetables give me a natural lift. Colors speak to me in the most elemental language—feelings, and in particular, my feelings—my instinctive response to colors.

At the outset, it's important to know that the Supermarket Test is based upon my belief that we will not like the color of anything if we don't also like its taste. Said another way: We like a color of a fruit or vegetable *only if we like its taste.*

I've found over the years in using this test with hundreds of clients, that taste plays a part in the subconscious reason we like a color. Have you ever thought about how we key color in our vocabulary to food in its natural state? Think a moment about the various names we give color. Lemon yellow. Plum. Lime green. Tomato red.

The Supermarket Test is based upon my belief that whatever we accept with our eyes first, we have subconsciously accepted into our bodies. And my research with my clients dramatically proves that if we're attracted to the color of a fruit or vegetable, we like its taste.

Why don't we eat worms or rats? The thought of eating a worm or a rat is repulsive to us. Yet the color of both of these creatures is very much like the color of mushrooms. Several years ago *House and Garden* magazine featured a new grayish-brown color. What did they call it? "Rat?" "Worm?" No, they called it "mushroom," because in truth the color was very much the same in tonal value as that of a worm or rat! *House and Garden* knew that no one would accept a color if it were named after something we wouldn't readily ingest. Therefore, rats and worms were out; "mushroom" was in. The magazine copywriters understood this basic color truth: We like the color of a fruit or vegetable *because we like the taste* of that fruit or vegetable.

When you've completed the Supermarket Test you'll see that we accept food of almost every color into our bodies. However, there are certain tones of colors that are missing from the supermarket test ground simply because all colors aren't found in natural produce, such as the lighter tones of the blue of the blueberry. Although no supermarket, no matter how vast and varied its produce, can show you every conceivable shade of every color, the Supermarket Test will introduce you to a broad spectrum of radiant tones of colors that will make your heart leap with joy.

So, to start:

Choose a time to take the Supermarket Test when you know you can be alone. Make certain your children are at school or out playing—anywhere but home! You'll need approximately an hour for the test.

Go to a market where fruits and vegetables are so beautifully displayed that they really do form an array of abundant color. Select the supermarket only on the basis of its fruit and vegetable display. Once you've chosen the place, follow every rule exactly as stated.

Supermarket Test Rules: Part One

1. To take this test you must surrender your mind, act instinctively, react emotionally, and trust your intuition. Do this test with a "no mind" attitude. You will learn at the end of this experiment that you *do know* which colors you will be happy living with. You'll also learn that you don't need an expert to select "your colors." You'll soon know without any doubt in your mind that you're your own best expert.

2. Take no one with you. No children, no spouse, not a friend; just you and enough money to allow you to check out a small cartful of color.

3. Keep your mind free of everything but this test. Don't think about errands you must run or what you need to do today. Walk into the supermarket with all your energies focused on taking this test, without a thought of anything else.

4. Free your mind of every old notion about which colors "go together". Don't think about whether the bunch of scallions you put in your cart will complement the eggplant or cherries you've just put into your basket. **REMEMBER**: You're allowing your emotions and your instincts to guide you.

5. Don't tell yourself, "I already have red radishes so I don't need a red tomato as well." Radishes and tomatoes are two very different reds. Pick up anything and everything that appeals to you and place it into your basket.

6. *Do look at* the rich colors of every variety of the produce. Feel, as well as see, the colors. Accept the colors in a spontaneous, childlike way and you'll find that you're beginning to discover that you have a natural association with the fruits and vegetables in that you "see" color and taste as one. For instance, if you see a cantaloupe, don't worry that you'll "see" the skin color of the melon. You won't. You will be "seeing" the edible color of the melon. To test this, ask a friend what color she "sees" when you say "pineapple." What color does she think of when you say "kiwi?" In both cases, the outer skin is a brownish color, but her response will be "yellow" and "green."

7. Systematically, pick up the vegetables and fruits that have colors that appeal to you, and place them in your cart. Walk up the produce aisles and then turn back and walk down them again—the second trip down the aisle you might see something you missed on your first trip.

You can be sure that your subconscious will do the tasting for you because your eyes will accept only the food that you like.

Now that you have picked up the fruits and vegetables and piled them into your cart, you've completed Part One of the test. You're now ready for Part Two.

Supermarket Test: Part Two

1. You've finished your shopping. Buy nothing else. Check out and go directly home. Don't stop for a conversation with a friend you haven't seen in weeks or make a quick stop at the bakery. Remember that you're taking a test.

2. Once home, turn your phone off. Give yourself total peace and quiet. This is essential because interruptions will destroy the effectiveness of this exercise.

3. Select 3 items: A large platter, a dinner-size plate—preferably white— and a knife.. Place all your vegetables and fruits into the sink and run water over all of them. You'll see that as the water splashes onto each of the fruits and vegetables their beautiful colors emerges. With the water still glistening on them place them on the platter.

4. Sit down at the table with your small plate, the large platter of fruits and vegetables, and the knife and fork.

5. Look the fruits and vegetables and select those with the colors you *most respond to* and that you instinctively *find most appealing*. Place them on the smaller plate. Take no more than a few seconds because after that time you'll be thinking—you'll be using your mind—rather than responding spontaneously.

In those first minutes you will know the colors you'll be happiest living with. In all probability they are the same colors you responded to and loved when you were a child, and these are the colors you will always love.

Look at what you chose. There might be a glistening romaine lettuce set off by a ripe persimmon. A black-purple eggplant or a sunny yellow squash. A scallion, an orange, a rich red beefsteak tomato. Whatever you've chosen, you will have produced a dazzling array of pure and natural color.

6.   Now slice through each of the fruits and vegetables. You'll see that the outer skin and the inside, together form the essence of the food.

I'll explain. We say "apple red," not "apple white," although it's the tart-sweetness of the inside of the apple that appeals to us. Nevertheless, since we've accepted the white of the apple, we've also accepted its red skin. In the case of the apple, the outside red becomes synonymous with the taste of the inside white flesh of the fruit. Color and taste blend and emerge as "apple red," a tone of red that we accept with our eyes—and that we ingest. Even though our taste preference may depend upon a special recipe for preparing the fruit or vegetable, our minds always connect with food in its raw state.

In the short time it will take you to complete this test, you'll discover not only the colors you love, but also that you've been conditioned to exclude color from your interior environment—your home and office. No matter whether you are twenty-five or seventy-five when you give yourself the gift of the Supermarket Test, you'll be able to reach deep within yourself and again find the colors that have special meaning for you. You'll have found your own colors.

Rediscovering why you like a color is always a fascinating experience. In my own case, I know that my favorite color is red and the various tones of red. I love it because for my eighth birthday my aunt bought me a beautiful rose-red taffeta party dress. I felt like the prettiest person in the world in that dress. And I've always loved every tint and shade of rose to red since that time. A wonderfully pleasant memory imprints a positive association with a color. This never fades no matter how many other happy experiences we have. They become our personal color memories.

After taking the Supermarket Test, one of my clients told me that she had chosen a red tomato. "But I certainly wouldn't ever use that color in my home," she said.

I asked her if she ever used red in her home and she told me that some years ago, when she first was married, she had. But she assured me that her taste had changed since then.

I asked her to think back on her childhood and, drawing from my own experience, asked if she had ever had a favorite outfit she especially loved to wear. Her face brightened, and she began to tell me about a dress her mother had bought for her when she was seven. She remembered every detail of it and described the pleats in the skirt. When I asked her what color the dress was, she told me it was red. When she realized what she had said, she laughed aloud. "Of course! It was a gorgeous red velvet and I wore it to a Christmas party at my grandmother's house!"

My client's house, by the way, didn't turn out to be completely red. But we did use that shade of red, her party dress red, as a secondary color with other colors she discovered were the colors she really loved.

As many times as I've asked my clients to take this test, I have never ceased to be amazed at how often I hear, "Well, yes, as a matter of fact, yellow was a favorite color of mine when I was a child. But I wouldn't want to use it in my home." Color memories are very potent in your adult lives.

Men who take the Supermarket Test will often remember that their fathers had a tie they loved which was—can you believe it—"absolutely this green." They hadn't thought about that color in years and wouldn't have if they hadn't selected a head of Bibb lettuce when taking the Supermarket Test. My research has brought me unexpected joy when working with male clients. Men, I've found, very much enjoy taking this test. They throw themselves into it enthusiastically and are delighted by the results.

Not surprisingly, I've found that my own greatest successes involving the Supermarket Test come when both husband and wife participate—individually, of course. Each makes exciting discoveries about themselves and about each other.

Most of us have succumbed to a neutral-color environment after years of having been told that white is right and beige is restful and the only way to go. When we pass up orange, red, purple and yellow to take the safe, neutral path, we've opted instead for bland choices because we're afraid to taste the joy of color—to in fact, color our lives.

In the thirty years I've been using the Supermarket Test with my clients, it's missed twice. The first is with a client who after taking the test wouldn't discuss her findings—her color choices with me—because her husband was in the next room and she was sure he was listening to our conversation. She knew that while she and I would be discussing the results of the test, he would be monitoring whatever she said. She told me afterwards that when I left their house he ridiculed her for taking the Supermarket Test.

The other failure involved a woman who was simply too concerned with her own image to allow herself to get into the spirit of the test. She worried that she might not select the colors she felt she "should" choose. It was easy for me to see that she felt inhibited by what others would think. When she finally did consent to take the test, I knew that it wouldn't work for her. And it didn't.

Usually the Supermarket Test proves to be a fun experience—and an overwhelming success. At the follow-up appointment with my clients, when we discuss the colors they selected during the test, I'm often surprised and delighted by the choices of those who had insisted that they wanted a predominately beige color scheme. The Supermarket Test proves to them that they truly prefer exciting, luscious colors—as well as beige.

I especially enjoy the reaction of a client who wanted me to design the interior of her new apartment in a high rise in Denver. From her floor-to-ceiling windows she delighted in a panoramic view of the city and the mountains. When I first suggested that she take the Supermarket Test, she told me that she thought she'd feel silly.

My client had very good taste and a well developed fashion sense. She loved clothes and knew what she looked best in—styles as well as color. Yet, although she used color beautifully on herself, her choice of color in her home was something else entirely.

As expected she began by telling me that she wanted the major colors in her home to be brown, beige, and off-white. Her floors were a light teak and she wanted those teakwood tones to be set off by chocolate brown velvet throw pillows. Additionally, she rhapsodized that she wanted to bring in caramels, vanillas, butterscotches, and champagne.

I'd heard this before. And it always sounded fattening.

I asked if she might consider using one of the colors she was wearing that day. Her black dress was highlighted with a rich turquoise and purple stripe.

"Purple? Turquoise?" she said incredulously. "Heavens no. I want to keep the backgrounds neutral so that all the color in the room will come from my paintings."

I again encouraged her to take the Supermarket Test, to determine if browns and beiges were—as she was convinced they were—her absolutely favorite colors. She did, and told me afterward that she surprised herself when she didn't feel silly or embarrassed going through the supermarket picking up only one fruit and vegetable. And that she was delighted with the results.

She followed the rules without thinking about her choices, and she did indeed, choose the colors she loved best. She was partial to brown, and of course, when I designed her home, brown was very much a part of the color scheme. But she also discovered the soft purple of the eggplant. And she fell in love with the red of a gorgeous red pepper. Thinking about these colors after she "discovered" them, she realized that as a child she had a soft, purple bathrobe she adored.

Whenever she put it on, she was certain she really was a lost princess who had mistakenly been taken in by a loving, but un-royal family. More color memories at work.

Over the years she outgrew her need for royalty, but the lure of purple lingered. Moreover, she learned an important fact about using color: Never limit yourself to any single color. If you devour oysters every chance you get, and start the day with a bowl of oatmeal, and if you are certain that you're crazy about beige—by all means, enjoy it. But why limit yourself to a one-color diet? Just a walk in the park will show you the miracle of awe-inspiring colors—color really is all around you. Your life is too colorful to be viewed monochromatically.

Nor should you worry that you might be in danger of having your home look like a gypsy tent after taking this Supermarket Test. It won't. What will happen is that you'll discover or rediscover those three or four colors you truly love. And in a short time after taking the test you'll find that you've become more sensitive to all colors. Your awareness of various shades of colors will increase, and, ultimately, you'll find yourself responding instinctively and spontaneously to colors that appeal to you.

Your Supermarket Test colors will always be the colors you'll enjoy living with in your home. In addition, your increased awareness of color in general will also lead you to explore other tones and shades you might not have considered before. An unexpected bonus will be that you'll realize as you experience the pleasure of responding to color again that you were awakening the spontaneity of the child in you. Not only will you know which colors are "yours," as time goes on you'll wonder how you ever lived without them.

You Really Are What You Eat!

After you take the Supermarket Test, list the fruits and vegetables you found you were attracted to.

List the fruits and vegetables that you brought home with you from the supermarket.

_____

_____

Now list the fruits and vegetables you selected for your small plate and sliced into.

_____

_____

The colors of these fruits and vegetables are *your true colors.*

You might also enjoy using the colors of the fruits and vegetables from the large platter as the secondary, or as accessory colors throughout your home. After all, you're attracted to these colors, too.

The colors you selected for the small plate are your true colors.

In the following chapters, you'll learn how to use all of *your colors* in your home.

To Note What You Want to Remember

Chapter Four
How to Become a Color Maven

Each of you would like to be a color maven, a person with impeccable taste who knows instinctively which colors work best together. Few are born with this gift. Instead, when faced with a choice of colors to use, you freeze, worrying aloud that you really don't know which color "goes with" another. What often happens is that you give up and hire professional mavens, interior designers, who then describe the colors that are "perfect for you." Some designers will tell you that unless you've had formal training in the science of color, you shouldn't even try to unravel the mystery of color. "Leave color selections to a professional," these professionals will tell you. And to make the point, the designer may present you with a stack of colorful fabric swatches to choose from which could be certain to send you off in confusion. Worse yet, you may be shown a "color wheel," a technical device that often baffles even experienced, accomplished interior designers. I believe that the color wheel contains more information than you'll ever need to know about color. Using a color wheel to decide which colors "go together" is like buying a computer for the sole purpose of making your own travel arrangements online. It's an exercise in overkill.

There was a time when I believed that choosing coordinating colors didn't have to be a confusing experience. I knew that there wasn't anything mysterious about mixing and matching colors. All that was needed was an easy system to help make color choices. There was only one problem: There was no color coordinating system available anywhere.

I first realized the need for a non-intimidating, easy to use color system after I moved from New York City to Arizona. I was thrilled with the brilliant blue sky and the rich colors of flowers in bloom all year long. But I was completely mystified when I found that except for throw pillows and art hanging on their walls, there was very little use of color inside Arizonans' homes. Beige was the color of choice. It ruled supreme. I couldn't understand why.

Then, as I began working with clients, I discovered that it was nearly impossible to talk to them about color. Here in Arizona where each day opened and closed with the most spectacular apricot, golden and plum sunrises and sunsets, few people lived with color in their homes. When I suggested that the colors they loved in their gardens be used inside their homes, they liked the concept but they didn't think they could actually live with "so much color". Beige was better. And besides that, they knew they'd grow "tired" of colors in their homes.

Another major concern I often heard was that the colors they liked wouldn't "go together". I soon learned that showing them large samples of fabrics in colors of their choice wasn't enough. They still saw beige as the most beautiful and the safeset color to use in their homes. I was convinced that what they needed was an easy method they could depend upon so that they would know beyond any doubt that the colors they loved in their gardens and the colors they chose after doing the Supermarket Test, they'd also love living with in their homes.

Eight years after I started working to develop a simple-to-use color matching system that would give my clients the confidence to choose the colors they loved *inside their homes*, I developed the Color Bars. I tested it hundreds of times, and it worked—every time. I'd done it. It was an absolutely foolproof color matching system!

The Color Bars is based on the tonal values of color, more technically referred to as shades (darker tones) or tints (lighter tones) of color. The Bars consist of 64 tones of every color. Thirty-two colors on one side of the Bars have even numbers, and thirty-two colors on the other side of the Bars have odd numbers. Ail odd numbered colors 1, 3, 5 and 7 are coordinated to each other and all even numbered colors 2, 4, 6 and 8 are coordinated to each other. Simply put: All Odd Numbers go with each other, and all Even Numbers go with each other. There is no way to make a color mistake. The Color Bars are absolutely foolproof!

The Color Bars allow you to choose the colors you would love to use in your home, and be certain that they'll be beautiful together. You can be sure they'll work with each other because all the colors are already coordinated for you. The colors match each other.

A primarily one-color theme is called a monochromatic color scheme. Have you ever been in a friend's home and found yourself in an all-blue world? Usually the blue will be relieved by judiciously placed white. Designing a room—or even an entire home—in shades and tints of a single color, a monochromatic color scheme, is often the choice of people who are uncertain about how to use color in their homes. It's true that blue on blue on blue (various tones of blue) is not "busy," but it's also true that this, or any one-color palette, quickly becomes cliche. Unrelieved sameness usually needs serious help.

Interior designers will often plan rooms or even entire homes in tints and shades of one color because they understand that their clients will more readily accept various tones of a single color in their homes; that their clients will feel that their homes won't be "busy" or that they'll grow tired of the colors.

We know that all blues, like all greens, are not created equal. To test this for yourself, think how you respond to different tones of a color. Think of the color Wedgwood blue. Can you associate any experience you've had with this color? Now mentally, place this tone of blue on the musical scale. How do you hear it—as a low or a high tone?

Think of the color navy blue. Can you associate any experience you've had with navy blue? Now mentally place this tone of blue on the musical scale. How do you hear it—as a low or a high tone?

From this simple exercise you should be able to see how differently you respond to each shade or tint of the same color. Color is so vivid in our minds that we can almost "hear" it. We will also associate a color with an experience we've had. In our color memories we "see" the event in color.

Yet we often banish a single color from our homes—thereby dismissing all the tones of that color. I cannot tell you how many times I've asked my clients the colors they'd like to use in their homes, only to be told, "I definitely don't like green" (or red, or orange, etc.) However, when I ask these clients how they feel about *apple* green or a *cucumber* green and I show it to them on the Color Bars, they find themselves accepting that an apple green or a deep green pillow would look good on their beige sofa. When I've shown them all of green's color possibilities—the range of tones of green—they will almost always become receptive. They understand then that it's not the color they don't like—it's the *tone of the color* they're reacting to. . At times almost all of us have or had similar responses to colors.

There are approximately 1,000 tones of every color. If we say we like or dislike yellow, for example, whether the yellow is a marigold yellow with orange in it, or sunflower yellow without a trace of orange in it, do we mean that we really dislike yellow—*all 1,000 tones of yellow?* When we say we dislike red, whether the red is a crimson tinged with blue, or a pure scarlet red, do we really dislike red—*all 1,000 tones of* red?

Think for just a moment what it would feel like to live in a home filled with only bright primary colors. Unrelieved by the in-between tones, primary colors feel too bright and too brittle in an interior environment. Because we all have a natural relationship with color, as you use the Color Bars, you'll experience a renewed connection to colors as you discover the shades and tints of colors you can confidently use.

I particularly remember Susan, who was planning to move to Phoenix from Seattle. Seattle, of course, is a rainy, cool, often cold city. And Phoenix is a dry, warm, often hot city. To bring warmth to her home in Seattle, Susan had decided to use a mostly yellow color scheme with white as the secondary color in the living room and dining room. I asked her what colors she was thinking of using in her new home in Phoenix. She told me that she loved the yellow and white color scheme but she realized that yellow was too warm a color to use in Phoenix. I assured her that she could use it.

I asked her if, in addition to yellow and white, had she considered using any other colors? She seemed uncertain, and said she never had.

I asked her to look at the colors on both sides of the Color Bars—both the Even numbered and the Odd numbered sides to see what other colors she liked enough to consider using them in her new home. After a few moments, she pointed to the number 6 green on the Color Bars. This was the same tone of green of the leaves in the plants in her living and dining rooms. The yellow in her fabrics were number 2 yellow on the Color Bars. Because even numbers go together on the Color Bars we had a perfect match. I then simply used the number 2 green (taken from the leaves of her plants) for her draperies in a geo-metric patterned fabric with the number 2 green background. I used the same fabric in a floor-length cloth on a round lamp table. And the same shade of green was repeated again in an area rug in the living room. With the mostly yellow fab-rics from her home in Seattle, Susan was amazed at how beautifully the green coordinated with it. The Color Bars enabled Susan to see that the tonal value of the number 2 yellow in her existing fabrics worked with the number 6 green.

Because of the lighting in her living room, I felt we needed still another color. Yellow, white, and green is a very good color scheme, but a fourth color was needed to compensate for the lack of natural light in her living room. Again I showed her the Color Bars, and we found just the right color—the number 4 red. The red was present in the geometric fabric I had used for the draperies and table covering, and now it appeared in many smaller ways—in a pair of red glass vases and other accessories.

Unlike as when we're in love, when we're designing a room, it takes more than two to create excitement. Often, however, people feel uncomfortable intro-ducing a third color into a room and are absolutely lost when thinking about bringing in a fourth. Instead, they lean toward the old, safe monochromatic color scheme. Or they choose a timid, tentative two-color design. When using the Color Bars, however, it's easy to add those third and fourth colors that turn a room from nice into knockout.

Putting Your Skills to Work with Your Personal Reaction Journal

You've taken the Supermarket Test to discover your true colors. You've considered the tonal values of the colors you want to use. You've followed the Odd and Even Color Bars system and decided which numbers of colors appeal to you. Now you're ready to become a full-fledged color maven. You're ready to use your new skills to bring radiantly beautiful color into your home.

Look around your room. You know you want to do something. But what? So that your room will ultimately look and feel the way you want it to, begin this project by asking yourself the following questions.

❖ What is it that you don't like about the room?

_____

❖ Is it the general style of the furnishings?

_____

❖ Is it the period of the furnishings?

_____

❖ Would you prefer French Country, Early American, English, Contemporary, or a Southwestern, more casual look?

_____

❖ Do you prefer a combination of styles and periods?

_____

If you aren't certain of the answers to any one or all of these questions, now's the time to look through your "Rooms I Love" folder. You'll find your answers in your folder.

Carefully evaluate the present look of your room. Do a quick, but thorough, inventory of what exists.

Are there any architectural features already in the room which have color or to which you can add color?

_____

Are you pleased with the color these features add?

_____

Can this color be easily changed, as the color of beams and moldings can be, or are they permanent—as a brick or stone fireplace is?

_____

List the color or colors of your flooring—carpeting, hard-surface flooring, area rugs.

_____

List the color or colors of your walls (wall covering or paint).

_____

List the color or colors of your window treatments—draperies, shutters, blinds, shades.

_____

List the color or colors of your furniture. This includes wood tones and painted furniture.

_____

List the major colors in your accessory pieces—lamp bases, lampshades, accessories, trims such as on an upholstered sofa, draperies and/or drapery tie-backs.

_____

Note your feelings about the mood in this room. Love it, it's okay, not sure but it doesn't feel right.

_____

List any shades (deep tones) or tints (light tones) of your favorite colors already in this room. List where these colors appear.

_____

Now take another look around your room. What is the predominant color you see in the backgrounds—the floors, walls, ceilings, and window treatments?

_____

The predominant color is your major color in the room.

Are you happy with this color?_____

_____

If not, which of these backgrounds would you most want to change?

_____

To introduce a new major color into your room, plan to use this color on at least one of your background surfaces—the walls, floor covering, window treatments, or floors. Ideally, this new major color should be on the backgrounds of two walls and the floor covering, or for the window treatments such as drapery fabric, shutters, or blinds. Two elements in a room with a single color will bring a cohesive blend to your room.

Visualize the colors you would like to see in this room. Remember you already know the colors you love—you've taken the Supermarket Test and know that you can live happily with these colors. Write down the colors you would like to use in this room.

_____

Finding Your Major, Anchor, and Accent Colors

The major, or predominant, color in a room sets the mood of the entire room. But it is likely that you would like to use two, three, or even four colors in the room. But, how do you decide which will be the major color?

Of course, there is no right or wrong answer to your color choices. At times you might instinctively know the color you would like to be dominant in the room. Although you may have narrowed your color choices, perhaps you aren't sure. At this time the Color Bars, will be invaluable to you because you can tack the colors to walls to view them. It's an excellent way to see colors in various lights. However, if you need to see colors in larger volume use fabric samples.

Obtain samples of fabrics 12" in length and 12" wide in the colors you're considering. Tack one of the fabric samples on a wall, hang another at the window, place one on the floor and another on a chair. Rotate the placement of these samples for a couple of day, so that you can see each color as it would look hung as draperies, covering a wall, used in carpet or as upholstery.

As the light in your room changes during the day and evening, so will the tone of the colors. If you wish, here is the perfect opportunity to involve your entire family. Invite everyone to participate because if these colors are for your family room or kitchen, every member of your family will be using this room. With each fabric color, specifically ask yourself if you'd like to have a sofa or a lounge chair in that color; whether you'd like to see that color on your walls, whether you could be happy with that color in draperies or at your windows, and whether you would like to walk on that color.

Keep track of all your answers. And remember: *white, off-white, and beige all count when you're choosing your major color.* If you're changing all the back-grounds in the room, the color you select for two of the backgrounds becomes your major color.

If you don't want to change your existing background colors, introduce your new major color in inexpensive ways. Usually this can be accomplished by painting the walls or ceiling, or both, and by bringing the new color into play in your window treatment as well. Again, your major color must occur in major ways in the room. It should appear on at least one of the vertical surfaces—walls or window treatment—and ideally, it should also appear on a horizontal surface.

Identifying your major color is easy when you're using a solid-colored fabric or other material. But things get trickier when you introduce patterns. The best rule for patterned fabrics is that your major color is the shade or tint that is predominant in the fabric. It's the color you see first. If you decide to introduce your major color in your window treatment, this color should be the dominant color in your draperies.

You may decide you would also enjoy sitting on the color you've chosen as the major color in the room. If so, plan to use it on a sofa and a chair as well as on a vertical background. By doing this, you use your major color in a big way, both horizontally and vertically.

Identifying Accent and Anchor Colors

Now that you know your major color, it's time to add accent colors and, if you've chosen a light tone as your major color, you can also add an anchor color. To select your accent colors, look at your fabric samples again. You can use shades or tints of any or all of them as accents. Refer again to your Supermarket Test and to the colors you identified as your true colors. Remember that all colors go with each other when they are of the same tonal value. Here is where your Color Bars will help you because it takes the guesswork out of choosing the right colors.

Pay attention to the patterned fabrics you consider for your backgrounds. Manufacturers do a lot of the work for you. So, as you browse through wall covering, floor covering, or fabric samples that use your major color in a big way and notice the tones of the other colors that appear. All of these can be used as accent colors in your room. This system, by the way, has a wonderful side benefit. In making color your guide, you establish a firm basis for making decisions as you begin to look at other fabrics, wall and floor coverings.

NOTE: Focusing on the colors you want to use will help you know where to begin when shopping for fabrics and materials. You begin with color. *Then* you look at pattern, fabric, and textures.

In contrast to your major color, **accent colors appear in less important ways in a room.** They may appear as dominant colors in patterned fabrics used on smaller pieces of furniture or in accessories such as pillows, area rugs, or lamp bases. Because accent colors add zest, life, and interest, the most successful schemes are those in which three, or even four colors are used in a room.

The anchor color is the deepest tone of any of your colors. Once you've identified this color, **use it abundantly** in your room. Use it in major pieces of upholstered furniture, in your accessories, in large pillows for your sofa, or in architectural features such as beams and/moldings. Plan also to use this deep tone in smaller ways, such as a painted table, or in the mats of framed pictures or the frames themselves. ***The anchor color should be almost, but not quite, as important as the major color.***

Putting Major Accent Colors to Work with the Anchor (Deep Tone) Color

Let's take a look now at a room that is designed around a deep shade of a major color. Picture a family room with oatmeal carpeting, off-white painted walls, brown and beige draperies that are only a year old and in excellent condition. There are also a large beige sofa, two lounge chairs, three tables and lamps, and a game table with four chairs. You are my client and you tell me that you want to add some zest to this room. You've taken the Supermarket Test and you use the Color Bars. You've worked with fabric samples to determine the colors you want to live with, and you and your family have decided on tangerine as your major color, with turquoise and tomato red as your accent colors. You may want to add other colors as well. But you don't have unlimited funds and you want to do this as inexpensively, yet effectively, as possible.

Begin by painting the window wall and the wall adjacent to it tangerine. It's especially important when choosing a deep shade as your major color to adhere to this rule: always paint at least two walls that deep tone. Keep the other wall or walls a light color. Never use *two different* deep tones of the same color for the four walls in any room!

The tangerine walls will contrast with the beige-brown draperies. Repeat the tangerine in the draperies by trimming them with a three-inch band of fabric with the same type or weave as the fabric of the draperies. If your draperies will traverse on rod, begin your trim at the top of the heading *behind the first pleat*; and run the band down the drapery and across the top of the hem, so that when the draperies are closed, the band trim will be visible and not lost in the fold of the drapery. Add a one-inch turquoise grosgrain ribbon against the three-inch tangerine band, placing it exactly as the three-inch band is placed on the drapery, behind the first pleat, and down the closure and across the top of the hem.

Since tangerine is a deep shade, you do not have to designate an anchor color. The deep tangerine anchors your color scheme.

You're not locked into your original three colors when choosing fabric for the room although the tangerine, turquoise and red should reappear in the room—but so can others! When you decide on a fabric, cover a couple of large 24" X 24" pillows in that fabric and place them on the beige sofa. You might also add somewhat smaller, 22" X 22" turquoise pillows to be placed in front of or next to the larger cushions. Trim the turquoise pillows with a border of tangerine grosgrain ribbon, and plan to use an odd rather than an even number of pillows on the sofa. Try adding a wide, flat pillow in tangerine, and place this against one of the turquoise pillows.

Have fun with your colors and the way you use them in your room. Frame your prints with colored mats. Spotlighting two or more black-and-white prints with quarter-inch turquoise mats, over which is placed a five or six-inch red mat. Frame the prints with simple molding. A favorite way I design prints is with a wide mat dressed up with a colorful quarter-inch lip of the existing mat.

NOTE: What's important is that the accent colors appear abundantly in both vertical and horizontal places in the room—on the walls and in the seating.

When you decide to make another major purchase, look for a rug in turquoise, red, and tangerine or with these colors in the pattern of the rug.

If you've decided to replace your sofa, here is your opportunity to introduce another fabric pattern into this room. Feel free to vary the size of the patterns you use in a room. If you used a small pattern on the chairs around the game table, you may want to use a larger pattern for the sofa. Very often introducing a second pattern allows you to bring in a new color. It's best to limit the number of patterns to two. Unless you've had success working with three or more patterns in a room before, leave this to the experts.

With a Tint (A Light Tone) As Your Major Color

When designing a room with a light color as your major color, choose an anchor color plus at least two additional colors for that room.

Example: If you've chosen the lighter tone of peach as your major color and you've decided that your accent colors are turquoise, white, yellow and a medium gray, the medium gray becomes your anchor color. Paint the walls and ceiling peach. Choose a patterned fabric with predominately peach colors for the draperies, and use this fabric on secondary seating (game chairs or occasional chairs) as well. The gray will be in your carpeting or an area rug on your hardwood or tile floors, and on major upholstered pieces such as your sofa and lounge chairs. The gray could also appear as the background color of the patterned fabric you introduce in smaller ways in this room. Use this fabric for a tablecloth and in sofa pillows. Turquoise and yellow become your accent colors and each of these colors should appear in less important ways in the room. For instance, upholster a small chair in turquoise, use yellow or turquoise lamp bases with white lampshades; add picture mats in lemon yellow. These colors could appear in an area rug and in collectables and accessories also.

REMINDER: Always count white, off-white, beige, and black as colors when making your color plans. Metal finishes such as chrome, brass, copper, or pewter work well with all colors in all tones and do not count as a color.

As you use the Color Bars you will discover that you are aware of an ever-increasing variety of shades and tints of color, and realize that choosing colors for your home is great fun!

Chapter Five
Myths, Truths, and Tips

Now that you've become a color maven and know your own colors, you're ready to take on some popular interior design myths that you've probably heard of and perhaps repeated as gospel. But the truth is often a very different matter.

How often have you been told that all rooms must "flow?"

Or that a home should follow a theme?

Or that the entrance to your home or foyer is "not that important"?

Below are a few of the most often repeated, most common interior design myths, and an explanation of why you should disregard them.

Myth: Art hung on the walls, and the accessories in the room, set the mood of the room.
Truth: Color is the key element that creates and sets the mood of every room.

Visualize the following: You walk into a room that has coral colored walls and white moldings. Does the coral and white in this room have an impact upon you? Do you feel the mood of this room?

Now visualize walking into a room with beige walls and white moldings. Does the beige and white in this room create another mood? Are you feeling the difference between the coral room and the beige room? Regardless of the art on the walls and the accessories, *color is always the key element that sets and creates the mood of a room.*

Myth: Rooms should "flow".
Truth: Rivers must flow. Your home is not a river.

We know that we experience more than one mood in a single day. More accurately, almost everyone experiences a minimum of three, more often several, unrelated and different moods in a single day. Therefore, since you experience a variety of moods every day, and because you want your home to reflect you, doesn't it stand to reason that your home should have more than one color "flowing" throughout it?

Color is the key element that creates the mood of a room, and therefore, a single color "flowing" in every room, has no place in your home. Instead, use color to treat each room individually so that when you enter a room you feel that it expresses another aspect of you.

In my own home I treat each room individually. The walls of every room has a different color. The dining room is a sunny yellow. The kitchen, where I spend a lot of happy time cooking for my family and friends has mango colored walls and robin's egg blue cabinets. Our bedroom is a rose color—moire fabric covers the walls in this color and the carpeting is rose as well.

Our family room flooring is hand-formed terra cotta tile, the living room floor is white scored concrete, and the dining room floor has an oak parquet floor inlaid with walnut. The kitchen flooring is hard wood planked cherry. I use carpeting only in the bedroom areas.

Although several rooms open onto the next room and the flooring materials abut to each other, visitors to our home tell us, "Your home such a warm and cozy feeling." No one has ever said, "Your home doesn't flow. How come?"

If you color-plan each room, your home will immediately give you the personal look you'll love living with. The colors, patterns and textures in your background surfaces—walls, floors, windows, window treatments, and ceilings—will very likely be different in every room. If you're wondering if your home will look "choppy," it won't. Using matching colors—coordinated colors—allows you to pull all the architectural elements and your furnishings together so that your home will have a cohesive look and feeling. Colors matched to each other—as they are in the Color Bars—will free you from the rigid rule of "flow."

TIP*:* Use color on architectural focal points—molding and beams—to create more interest in a room. Using one color throughout your home creates sameness and sameness makes for a cliché home.

Myth: **Textures should be all of a kind.**
Truth: Mixed textures are dramatic and always an unexpected delight to see and touch.

The key to mixing fabric textures within a room is found in the types of fabrics you use. The fiber of a fabric—whether it's cotton, silk, linen, or synthetic—is as important as the weave of those fibers. Always, it's the weave of the fabric that creates its texture. Because man-made fibers are woven on looms similar to those used for natural fibers, many less-expensive synthetic fabrics have textures similar to natural fiber fabrics. The looms are so good that often polyester and natural-fiber fabrics are difficult to tell apart.

So take advantage of this unexpected benefit of technology and have fun using and mixing fabrics that have a variety of textures. Large, soft linen pillows on your silk sofa will look smashing. Or flank your velvet sofa with two soft, butter suede chairs. These two textures, velvet and suede, used closely together complement each other beautifully. Both of these materials are available in the most glowing and gorgeous colors. The synthetic "suede" is wonderful for upholstery and is a fraction of the cost of natural suede and of course, is also available in the most luscious colors.

It's important to know that natural materials are always harmonious when they're used together. Their textures are always a complement to each other, and because suede, linen, silk, and leather and cotton are natural fabrics and materials, you can use them together in your rooms with confidence.

TIP: It's a myth that certain fabrics are dressy or tailored. Silk is not necessarily a dressy or more formal fabric. Nor is linen a more casual, informal fabric. How a fabric is used determines its look.

When mixing textured materials and fabrics, the Color Bars will enable you to make accurate color decisions.

TIP: Mix textures of sofas and throw pillows together by trimming the pillows with the sofa fabric, and vice versa.

Myth: **Ceilings must be white or much lighter in color than the walls are.**

Truth: Light reflected from the ceiling is insignificant.

Ceilings are very often the forgotten elements in rooms; however, they offer an excellent opportunity to add variety, space, and vitality to any environment. A ceiling in a color that is different than the color of the walls in that room will draw your eye to the space above your head—and thus visually decrease the size of the room.

People have been conditioned to believe that white ceilings create more light and the illusion of added space in a room. In truth, that's not so. A room will not appear to be longer, wider or higher when the ceiling is white, and the white ceiling doesn't lend a room any more additional light than it already has. The room remains just what it is: a room with a white ceiling.

Major Truth: Paint your ceiling the same color as the walls. Because we see far more than we realize from our peripheral vision, your room will give the impression of having larger dimensions when the ceiling and walls are the same color.

This is because when the wall and ceiling colors are identical, the eye doesn't stop at the top of the wall before it moves to the ceiling, and therefore, a fool-the-eye impression occurs to us and the room *appears to be larger.*

There are times when the design of a room calls for a ceiling in a color completely different from the wall color. For Example: You might choose a deep, azure blue for your ceiling and accent it by painting the beams and the walls a chalk white. Upholster your sofa in an azure blue fabric—the same color as the ceiling. Add large (22" and 24" square) hot pink, emerald green, and coral pillows for your sofa and lounge chairs. Your floors could be hardwood in a medium to dark brown stain. With an area rug in colors compatible with the colors in the room, you'll have created an inviting and beautiful room. In this case, you've anchored the blue ceiling by repeating the blue on the sofa.

TIP: In both small and large rooms, for a cohesive and harmonious look, paint the ceilings and the walls the same color.

Myth: **Only big is beautiful.**
Truth: Small is also beautiful.

Small rooms can become the jewel. We often hear and read that white expands a room. But in fact it doesn't. Instead, reach for deep-toned rich colors of when designing a small room. If you want to use a patterned fabric, choose one with a rich jewel-tone background and use this patterned fabric lavishly.

One of the most charming rooms I've designed was a "room of her own" in a New York City apartment. It was situated at the end of a bedroom hallway and was, in my client's words, an "extra room" they used to store their suitcases and boxes of old tax records. She wanted to have a room of her own where she would have her books, her desk; that it be more her own retreat.

I upholstered the walls of this small room with a typical Persian paisley patterned fabric. I used the same fabric on the ceiling, and draped it in a shallow tent design. I used the paisley design again for the daybed, and accented it with brass nail heads. I selected the green in the paisley for velvet to upholster a small French wood-framed chair and footstool. Large throw pillows of paisley and velvet were placed on both the daybed and the chair. Paisley drapery panels hung at the windows. The draperies were dressed with a small, straight valance. The valance and the draperies were trimmed with 1-inch wide green grosgrain ribbon at the closure and along the top of the hem. The 3-inch wide tiebacks were also trimmed with grosgrain ribbon. Behind the draperies, a Roman shade of the same paisley fabric added privacy to the room.

The use of the single dramatic print fabric transformed what had been an unused "extra room" into a much-loved, much-used jewel of a room.

TIP*:* Large fabric patterns in several colors in small rooms are dramatic. A fabric with a pattern repeat of up to twenty-seven inches can bring that wonderful jewel-of-a-room-look to a small room. Limit to two the number of solid colors you use in a small room. To make your color choices the Color Bars will be of great value to you.

Myth: **A black-and-white color scheme is hard to live with.**
Truth: Using black and white together is beautiful and when done skillfully is easy to live with.

This color scheme is rarely used well because a hard-edged look is usually the result. Yet, far from being hard to live with, black and white create a powerful and exciting color scheme. When you add a third solid color as an accent color in your room, the black and white will spring to life, and soften the sharpness of the black and white combination and the room will become surprisingly inviting.

When working with black and white, make certain that the background color of all the black-and-white patterned fabrics you're using in your room is always the same. For example, if black is the background on a black-and-white patterned fabric used for the chair, black must also be the background for the patterned wall covering you may be using. Feel free to mix and match two pattern combinations in an average-sized room, adding your own favorite third color as a strong accent. If the room is larger than 17 feet wide and 25 feet long, the background color in another patterned fabric can be changed to white. Large rooms give us greater freedom to make choices.

TIP: In a smaller room, perhaps one that is 15 x 17 feet, you'll find that a black and white stripe as your third pattern can easily be added in a small way—to upholster the seat of a bench or footstool, or for throw pillows. Introduce this third pattern in a small way—on a bench or footstool or throw pillows.

Myth: **Homes should follow a theme.**
Truth: Homes that follow a theme look self-conscious and contrived.

Homes with one theme are like people with one topic of conversation— very boring. You know before you see them precisely what they'll be talking about. To avoid the "theme" look apply the fashion rule of mix-and-match to your home. When you mix and match styles and periods, patterns and furnishings, your home will reflect the real you. As you grow in experiences your home will mirror you. It will have your personality and *feel like you.*

Myth: **Foyers are "not that important."**
Truth: Foyers are the introduction to your home. For that reason they're very important.

Pay special attention to your foyer. When you think of colors for your foyer or the entrance to your home, choose softer tones of the major color you 're using in the next room. A soft color has an especially attractive and more welcoming feel to a home.

TIP*:* A foyer is the perfect place for one very important-sized piece of furniture. Here, big truly is beautiful!

Hang a large, framed mirror on the important wall of this room and position a handsome plant or tree in a handsome container in the corner. Or hang one large picture—a painting or lithograph—in your entranceway. But don't hang several small pictures on the walls of the entrance to your home. Lots of little *anything* should never appear in the foyer. And of course, a console table or chest is always gracious.

Myth: **It is very hard to find a place for painted furniture in a home.**
Truth: Fine painted furniture brings wood tones to life.

Painted furniture is every bit as attractive and important as furniture finished in wood tones. Don't exile your painted furniture to a seldom used bedroom. Instead place it in an important room of your home, and discover the beauty of fresh color that painted furniture imparts to any room.

Painted furniture creates a completely unexpected focal point and adds a mood of spontaneity to a room. Even when painted furniture is categorized as folk art, it somehow carries with it a sophisticated feel and brings with it an echo of delicious whimsy.

TIP*:* Most amateur do-it-yourself furniture finishers aren't capable of duplicating the craftsmanship required to produce fine painted furniture. These pieces are painted and then hand glazed and hand rubbed. A single piece of fine painted furniture is labor-intensive and entails several processes that often require two or three colors, and three or four coats of paint to achieve that special look.

As you see, color is very often the key ingredient that dispels a myth and creates a truth. As you develop the full color personality of your home, you'll free yourself from feeling bound by any rigid interior design myths, and you'll discover that old myths have no place in your new, colorful life.

Chapter Six
You and Your Child

One of the least-considered and most important things you can do for your child is this: Allow your child to create his own environment. There is more psychological back-rubbing, more "making nice," and more positive stroking involved in letting your child create his own room than in just about anything else that you might do for him. Yet parents rarely give a child's room much thought. Instead, when a toddler outgrows the crib, mother and father buy him a bed and bedspread. That bed, plus a few shelves for his books and toys, becomes the child's personal environment. The room serves him through his preschool and early school years. Then when the child reaches nine or ten, a larger desk and a new bedspread might be purchased for him. The child's room may not be thought about again until he becomes a teenager. Then another overhaul might be considered.

At both of these times in an older child's life—age nine to ten and thirteen to sixteen—a child's room becomes the subject of parental attention. Mother may call in a professional designer, or she may decide to do the room herself. In either case, the child is usually asked his/her opinion after the fact—when the room has been redone. Rarely is a child actually involved in the planning of his own room, and even less often is the child allowed to create his own special, private space.

Discussion about your child's room can provide enormous opportunities for parent-child communication. Yet few parents recognize this. Instead they take for granted that children will live in homes created solely by adults. Consequently, although children know much about what their parents like, parents rarely know what their children might really like. Ask a small child about his home and he'll tell you, "Mommy loves our house." There is an implied belief in this communication: because Mommy made it, therefore Mommy loves it and it's good.

When children are surrounded by what they assume is our taste, they learn a lot about us from what they see. Of course, most adults don't feel it necessary to discuss carpets, draperies, and furnishings with a seven-year old. Even if a mother is unhappy with the way her living room appears, or wishes she could replace the faded living room draperies, her child remains insulated from her negative thoughts about her home. Mothers want their youngsters to be happy; they don't want to pass on negative feelings. Consequently, young children think their homes are beautiful regardless of how they appear to adults.

Such whole-hearted acceptance doesn't necessarily imply that young children mimic adult preferences. Indeed, many children—if asked—have distinctly different taste from their parents. But adults, who intellectually accept that each child is an individual and not an extension of themselves, emotionally have difficulty making this break. Instead, we assume that if we like a certain style, pattern or color in our home, so will our children.

Intellectually we accept that each child is an individual and not an extension of ourselves, yet emotionally we haven't made this break.

Few parents stop to realize that a child's room is his world. His room holds most of the possessions that are near and dear to him. It's where he feels secure when his light is turned off and it's now dark; when the night sounds have begun and he must go to sleep. His room is his refuge when he's upset, his haven when he's tired, his entertainment and rejuvenation center.

In his private bedtime hours he reaffirms that everything in his room was chosen and planned by him.

When a child's room is created by him, instead of for him, he gains in confidence. And he validates his belief in himself.

For more than two decades, the child's room has taken on additional significance. Society has changed. Many families move once every five years. Divorce and remarriage create blended families—his, hers, and theirs. A child's room may represent the only place of security in his constantly shifting life. No matter where he lives—or with whom he lives, when he's surrounded by an environment and objects he's selected, enveloped in colors he's chosen, a child will realize a much needed sense of stability. In these times it is important to consider that a child's room may be the only fixed point of identity for him in an unstable world.

Just two or three generations ago, children were born and raised, and even married in the same home, under the guidance, love, and protection of the same set of parents. A child's room, while necessary to his sense of self, was then only one more link in his familiar network. Yet how many children, even in those "best of times," were allowed to create their own environments? Not many. It's important to remember that those were also the days when children were "seen and not heard."

Today, your child's room can provide you with a wonderful opportunity to learn more about him than you may now think. His room will be a window through which you'll see his thoughts and dreams. Once you accept that your child's room is his own special domain, creating that room will be a meaningful experience for both of you. By allowing your child to select his colors and furnishings, you'll work with him as a guide rather than as a benevolent ruler.

When I explain this philosophy to my clients, one question comes up repeatedly. "How can I turn decisions about color and style over to a ten-year-old?" a mother will ask. "After all," she says, "children change their minds so easily."

That may be true, I tell them, but working with children who are creating their own rooms has shown me that they are among my most decisive clients.

They make up their minds quickly, and once they've made a decision they stay with it. In addition, children are very reasonable. When they're shown actual reasons why they need to select furnishings that will grow with them, they easily understand. It's then that we see their instinctively practical personalities emerge.

However, having said all this, we don't give a child *carte blanche*. The adult must guide the children in making decisions that will prove to be practical, aesthetically pleasing, and functional, now as well as through their high school years. I've found that when given the opportunity to make choices that will work well for them, practicality is rarely a problem.

So, where to begin? The logical place to start is with the child. At a very early age children show their true colors. They know instinctively which colors they love and want to live with, because they view color without fear or prejudice. They've not yet learned to be concerned or fearful that colors won't match or that they'll clash, so they respond naturally and intuitively to colors.

Even when two children are going to share a single room, I begin by interviewing each child individually, before discussing any design concepts. Children can readily tell you what they want their rooms to look like if you ask them. But they must feel free to speak candidly.

At the outset I explain to parents that I prefer to speak to each child alone, preferably without mother or father present. Fathers usually accept this easily. Frequently, however, mothers want to be there to "hear what 'Ashley' has to say". In actual fact, I find they want to censor choices and ideas that don't match their own. At first, almost every parent is delighted to arrange such an interview for me. Involving their child is seen, initially by them, as charming, non-threatening, and avant-garde.

"Before we make this appointment," I will say, "I want you to understand that I need to hear what *Ashley* likes." I emphasize that this is why I prefer to speak to Ashley alone without any adults present. The parents agree, and we make an appointment at my studio. Ashley comes in—and her mother comes in with her. Both of them sit down, expectantly. I always sense mixed vibrations of apprehension and anticipation from both mother and child. At first the child is not sure just what is expected of her. But within minutes she relaxes and becomes involved in the interview.

Ashley answers naturally and easily. The nine-year-old is visibly excited by the prospect of creating her own room. Usually her mother is already thinking about the cost. As we begin the interview, I ask Ashley questions and she answers readily. As long as her mother is in the room, even if her mother does not interrupt her, she continually looks to her mother for confirmation.

She will answer my question, look up at her mother and smile, "Isn't that right?"

Mother doesn't have to say a word. Ashley immediately knows what her mother is thinking. At nine, she has developed an ability to hear a special frequency in her head that sends messages to her as surely as those that travel over radio waves. Just as she hears AM and FM on her radio, she hears "GM"—the "Great Mother" frequency. This station quickly tells her whether or not her answers are correct. If what she likes and wants in her bedroom doesn't meet with her mother's approval, Ashley immediately senses that she has somehow given a wrong reply. She picks up her mother's thought waves, she feels her mother's discomfort, she notices her mother's raised eyebrow, sees the slight frown between her mother's brows. She knows that she is "wrong." Within fifteen minutes of receiving these signals, the child's enthusiasm for choosing the colors and the mood for her room is noticeably dampened. By the end of forty-five minutes, Ashley's interest and confidence are gone.

What has happened? Ashley's mother begins with the best of intentions. She wants her child to have a "perfectly beautiful room," the one that she herself never quite had. No matter how lovely her own childhood room had been, she always knew that her mother created her childhood room, and that it had never looked the way she wanted or imagined her room to be. Yet, in her mind, Ashley's mother has pretty much chosen the fabrics and furnishings for her daughter's room. What's more, as her own mother had, she's already determined Ashley's needs.

Ashley's mother is a caring parent. She loves her little girl and wants only the best for her. There is one thing, however, that she hasn't considered. What does her little girl want?

She remembers that when Ashley was four, the nursery school teacher commented that Ashley used a lot of purple in her drawings. Her mother remembers that she thought this was unusual, since she had done Ashley's nursery in lime green and white. She had simply assumed that she would be drawn to those colors. Although she's never mentioned this to Ashley, she has planned a persimmon, white and lime green color scheme.

Ashley tells me, "I like purple." Her mother sends her a loaded look. The message the child receives is "that's a terrible color." From that look on, the interview goes down hill. Without meaning to, Ashley's mother has planted doubt in her daughter's mind and her daughter no longer feels confident about the color she likes.

Ashley's mother sincerely believes that she is encouraging her child to be creative. After all, she's arranged the interview with the interior designer. She's told her daughter to begin thinking about what she wants in her bedroom. She's even shown her some of her own favorite rooms in magazines. She would be appalled to hear that in fact, she is allowing Ashley to create her bedroom under her mother's shadow. Yet that is precisely what she is doing, and sending this message, loud and clear, on station "GM."

I find it interesting that fathers, generally, haven't developed such a frequency. The majority of men allow their children freedom to choose colors and furnishings for their bedrooms. Fathers rarely challenge their children's taste preferences. They rarely ask their children to reconsider their color choices. They don't tell a child that he or she is wrong. Even more revealing, fathers usually aren't as concerned with price, although certainly they'll be at least partially involved in paying for the new room.

Why the difference in mother and father's attitudes? I believe that it's because traditionally, the home has been mother's territory. His office or place of business is the father's domain. Although two-career marriages and incomes have become standard and the norm in our society, and while father is consulted and his opinion considered, hearth and home are still largely a woman's domain.

Since the man is not deeply involved in interior design decisions, he doesn't feel that his territory has been invaded by his child's decisions. As for his reaction to the price, men are accustomed to dealing with the total bill. Therefore, fathers rarely focus on each individual item.

There is a way to turn this heavy parental influence into a lifetime asset. By working with your child using the Personal Reaction Journal in this chapter you can discover your child's wants and needs. Together you'll create your child's room to meet her special needs. Far from being a censor or an all-knowing adult, you and your child will become partners in the process. And you'll also learn so much more than you now realize there is to know about your child. You'll treasure the insights you're about to discover. And once you know how to work with your child, you'll find that helping him create his own room will be a satisfying, creative, and great fun experience for both of you.

To begin with, remember one basic rule: *Never ask a question that can be answered with a simple "yes" or "no."*

Children must be encouraged to talk. Frame your questions to stimulate a complete response. Ask their opinions and be prepared to *listen to their answers.* Take the time to sit down with your child where neither of you will be disturbed. Select a place where you're both comfortable, and a time when there will be no interruptions. Make certain that you and your child are alone with each other.

It's important for children to understand why they must select furnishings that will grow with them. This is a difficult concept for young children to grasp because they don't have a frame of reference for what it means to actually be a bigger person. They know only what their size is now and what it felt like to be smaller. It's important and necessary to actually demonstrate to them what will result, as their bodies grow larger. They need to see that since they'll take up more space, they'll need larger size furniture. A teenager knows what it had been like to be seven; but a seven-year-old has no idea what it will feel like to be thirteen.

That's where measuring comes in. Children love to be measured. Have a yardstick or a measuring tape handy so that you can answer the following questions exactly.

To get the full benefit of this exercise, you and your child should do it together. Participation by both of you is key. If possible, girls should be measured against their mothers; boys against their fathers, otherwise, always measure a boy against a man, a girl against a woman.

1. What is your child's height?

_____

2. What is your height?

_____

3. How wide are her hips?

_____

4. How wide are your hips?

_____

5. Have her place her fingertips together, elbows pointing out and measure the distance from elbow to elbow. Let your child read the measurement so that she'll know how much space she now needs at a desk.

6. Place your fingertips together, elbows pointing out and measure the distance from elbow to elbow. This illustrates how much space you need at a desk. Let your child read the measurement to you. She will be amazed at how much bigger she is going to grow. This simple exercise is visual proof of something she realizes intellectually—but cannot now quite grasp: That, as she grows larger she'll require more space.

NOTE: It's important to explain to your child that a girl will often reach her full height by the time she's thirteen or fourteen. Although she won't be an adult, she'll have reached her adult size.

7. On paper show the total space the child requires today when she's sitting on a chair (hip measurement). And show the space she now needs at her desk (elbow measurement). Using your measurements, compare this with the space she'll need when she is an adult size. This will give her an immediate sense of why she must select furniture that will "grow" with her; furniture that is scaled for her size today and that she'll be comfortable with when she's your size.

Ask your child what colors he likes. Don't be surprised if he says, "I like all colors." Have him close his eyes and tell you the color he "sees." He may tell you he sees only two colors. Write them down.

_____

Ask him, "What do you think of when you see these colors"? Write his response down.

_____

Ask your child to close his eyes again. Tell him to imagine that he's in his bedroom and he's looking at his closet. Ask what he sees. Usually, boys and girls "see" their closet doors open. Little girls see their dresses and their shoes in that closet; little boys usually see only their shoes. Write down your child's description.

_____

_____

With his eyes closed, have him select one of the two colors he saw in his bedroom, and tell you where he'd like to have that color in his room. Boys will usually put color on the ceiling. Girls will usually see color on vertical surfaces. Ask your child how he feels about this color. He may tell you that it's OK, but that he wants it darker or lighter. Tell him that's fine. Young children, age eight to ten, enjoy this excercise. It's a game, and they think it's fun. What's more, once this room becomes a reality, they know it has their colors. It's really their room. Write down the colors and describe the tones of the colors they saw.

_____

If you're working with the Color Bars you'll find that children will be seriously considering all 64 colors. You'll find that your child will identify the colors he saw when he imagined his favorite colors in his room and he will choose the exact colors from the Color Bars.

He has now told you the colors he wants in his room. Don't worry that he might change his mind next week. He won't. Children are definite about color.

Many parents worry that young children will choose colors that are "terrible". In fact, this doesn't happen. However, little boys do love black, but that's not a terrible color and can be easily used in their rooms without their mother thinking it's terrible. They don't choose pink for their rooms because by age ten they're conditioned to think that pink is for girls. Also, children usually don't select wood tones or beige tones. They choose pure, exciting colors.

A child knows instinctively that there are no "wrong colors" for his or her room. There are plenty of theories that color experts purport, theories which, fortunately, most children have never heard of.

One noted color expert, for instance, states that yellow should never be used in a child's nursery. Yellow, he says, creates a nervous, anxious child. He claims that yellow drains creativity from an individual. This is nonsense. My extensive studies of color and its effects on people prove that yellow is a soothing, delightful color. Yellow is the color of tulips and daffodils and sunshine is often described as yellow.

I did my daughter's nursery in yellow. She was a happy and calm baby, and today is an optimistic, creative, and accomplished adult.

Red is another maligned color. Red is supposed to be a vibrating color that creates agitation in an environment. This is not so.

Navy blue is another taboo in a child's nursery. It's considered to be too somber.

My own experience continually flies in the face of what the color experts say. There is only one rule for using color: Live with what you like.

I did a nursery for a client's newborn child in all the "wrong" colors. We used a fabric in tones of bright navy blue, yellow, and red. When the child was eight her mother allowed her to redo her room. Although she changed the floral pattern to a geometric, she told me that she wanted to keep the "exact same colors." Today she is an intelligent eleven-year-old who logically arbitrates arguments between her two older brothers. Her mother describes her as having "a sunny and happy disposition."

Certainly, I don't claim to be partially responsible for why she's grown up this way. The colors of nursery room fabric doesn't provide the answer to a child's development. Her mother chose the colors for her nursery when she was barely weeks old with love and care. The fabric we used had a navy background, bright yellow tulips, and a vibrant tinge of red. We found the pattern charming.

The fabric she chose a few years later is a navy blue, red, yellow and leaf green geometric. She added bright green and loves the colors in her room. So, by the way, do I.

I believe that if you love yellow, it will not make you feel nervous. If you find red wonderful, it will not make you feel angry or aggressive. If you like the colors you choose for your child's nursery, you will feel happy using these colors, and your happiness will emanate into your child's room, and to your child.

Even if you use black, you'll use it appropriately and with joy. What's wrong with a black-and-white polka-dotted clown? When you approach a room with love and joy, undoubtedly you will choose colors that reflect those warm emotions.

Now that you know what colors your child wants in his room, you are ready to find out more about him and what else he wants in that room. "And a little child shall lead you" is a good mantra to remember as you work with your child.

Here are some questions for you to ask your child. Again, find time when neither of you will be interrupted. Write down his answers.

How much time do you spend in your room?

_____

What hours do you spend there in the morning, afternoon, evening?

_____

Which hours do you spend in your room on weekends? Morning? Afternoon? Before dinner? After dinner?

_____

_____

Do you spend any time in your room after you come home from school?

_____

How much time do you spend doing your homework in your room?

_____

How much time do you spend on the telephone?

_____

How much time do you spend on the computer?

_____

If your child will be allowed to have a telephone in his room, where would you like it to be placed? This is an important question because the question will usually open a new dialogue between you that you've never had before.

_____

_____

If you could have your room look exactly as you would like it, how would it look?

_____

_____

How do you feel about hanging up your clothes? Have you thought of an easier way to hang some of them—perhaps on hooks?

_____

_____

What do you like to do in your room? Play games, draw or paint pictures, read? List everything you can think of—nothing is silly or unimportant. Can you do it there easily, or do you need a special space for that activity?

_____

_____

If you share a room with your brother or sister, what do you think your room should have that would make you both happier in your room?

_____

_____

Describe how you would like your bed to look?

_____

_____

Once you've discovered what each child likes, shared bedrooms do not have to be problem areas. Because all colors go together, you will find that you can easily incorporate each child's favorite color into the room. Remember that a shared bedroom is still *each child's own individual room.* Every child needs privacy, a place to call his own. The size of the room has little to do with creating this atmosphere. How the individual child's space is used is what counts.

I find that when two children share a bedroom turning that single room into two "halves" works well. There are several ways to accomplish this that will work in small rooms as well as larger ones. Once you have each child answer the questions we discussed, you'll have a better understanding of the two individuals who share the space. Many families find that children actually prefer to share a room with a sibling.

——And For Your Entire Family——

Remember, too, there is additional important information to consider when designing any room in your home that your children use extensively. These can include a playroom, den, or family room.

Because after all, this is the entire family's home, each member of the family should be consulted. Ask each person in your family for an opinion individually before you begin designing a game room or family room. Make certain that each member of the family takes the time to write down his answers.

Ask each person to visualize what he or she would like to see in the room.

_____

_____

_____

Ask each person to visualize the colors he sees in that room.

_____

_____

_____

Ask each family member to identify a special need that he would like the room to accommodate such as: TV, board and card games, computer, etc.

_____

_____

_____

If each person could have anything he/she wanted in that room, what would it be? Have each take some time before answering this question; let your imagination soar. You may be surprised to find that turning dreams into reality can often be done with a minimum of cost.

_____

_____

_____

Encourage each member of the family to answer these questions. Then, when everyone has written his opinions, share the answers. You may be surprised at how easy it is to incorporate everyone's ideas into a family gathering place. Best of all, every member of the family will take pride in the completed room, because each person played an important role in creating it.

To Note What You Want to Remember

Chapter Seven
How to Create THE SENSUOUS BEDROOM

Although a *sensuous bedroom* awakens all your senses, it's not a sexy-looking bedroom. And a sexy-looking bedroom, very likely, is not a sensuous bedroom. The most beautiful sensuous bedrooms only imply and beckon—but they are never obvious. The sensuous bedroom hints of romance and *affaire d'amour,* and of delicious evenings and afternoons together.

And, although the rest of your home may be furnished in 21st century contemporary, or in 18th century European antiques, your bedroom should have a different feeling. Because the adult bedroom is also that room where intimate encounters between two adults take place, where hopes of fulfilling sexual desires happens, this room serves quite another purpose than does any other room in your home.

Although the adult bedroom has the requisite features of other bedrooms, it's a misconception that it is like other bedrooms. It's not. The adult bedroom serves very different purposes than children's bedrooms do. In fact, the adult bedroom is in a large sense the most unique room in your home.

Living rooms and dining rooms are where families congregate to discuss the day's events, finances, and plan vacations. But the adult bedroom is a hideaway, a private retreat. The adult bedroom is where endearments are whispered, where touching is a secret language, and where all your senses are awakened.

Yet, because all bedrooms are intensely private spaces, they must also be secure environments. As children we snuggled into our beds, wrapped in soft blankets, kissed by parents who promised us that we were safe from harm. As adults we view our bedrooms as places that extend those safe, soothing childhood moments. A favorite pillow, the texture of a blanket, the required firmness or softness of the mattress—all these are necessary for our adult security and serenity.

But adults' bedrooms have one important difference. A grown-up bedroom is also a playground for games that only adults can play. A sensuous bedroom *subtly signals* that games are accepted here. And while no one is pressured to perform, the message is clear. This is a room where usual and everyday proprieties are not expected: Where we nurture each other in the most intimate ways.

Yet a sensuous bedroom is never obvious. It never entraps or ensnares. Rather, it's inviting and exciting, suggesting; never making demands. To put this in perspective, a truly sensuous bedroom is a soft summer night; never a New Year's Eve.

Think about this for a moment. Your bedroom is the only room in your home for which you dress differently than you do for your kitchen, dining or living room. It's the only room in your house for which you have a completely different wardrobe. Where you wear sheer nightgowns or pajamas—or nothing at all. Taking all these factors into consideration, doesn't it make sense then, that your bedroom should also have a wardrobe different from that of the rest of the house?

By now you are probably mentally walking through your bedroom trying to decide if it's sensuous or not. If you have to think about it for very long, chances are yours is not a sensuous bedroom. You may have added some sensuous touches, perhaps masses of pillows, but unless the colors and the fabrics, and the patterns of those fabrics all work together, you've not achieved a sensuous look.

My client had draped her and her husband's bed with soft fabric, which can create a sensuous mood, yet the soft fabric had a bold, geometric pattern. The softness of the fabric signaled "yes," but the pattern of the fabric signaled, "no." My client didn't understand that a hard-edged geometric can never be sensuous. She told me she had wanted to design a *somewhat* sensuous bedroom and she failed, because designing a sensuous bedroom is akin to being pregnant: There isn't any way you can be somewhat pregnant. You either are, or you aren't. It's an all the way deal.

My client and her husband listened intently when we began talking about their bedroom, and they looked at it now with newly critical eyes. "You're right," they said, surveying the hard-edged geometric pattern. "Bring on the fabrics!"

This couple agreed that they wanted a beautiful, sensuous bedroom; yet they wanted one that would suit their practical and personal needs. He had his desk there, and both were avid readers. Their bookcase was filled with volumes that ranged from gardening to histories and mysteries. Their newly sensuous bedroom had to include both the desk, the bookcase, and comfortable seating.

They wanted every convenience they enjoyed in their former bedroom to remain at their fingertips in their new, sensuous setting.

To create this room for them, I had their walls sheathed in a combination of bronze mirror and a cantaloupe-colored soft cotton fabric. Instead of the tight, looped carpet they had, I used thickly piled carpeting in the color and tone of the wall fabric. I replaced the geometric-patterned bedspread with a down comforter/duvet and covered it in a lovely soft floral pattern. This fabric was in tones of cantaloupe and coral on a rich, deep emerald green background. I also covered several large pillows with the pattern, and repeated it again in floor to ceiling draperies at the corners of the bed, and at the windows.

I replaced their contemporary chrome lamps with porcelain lamp bases and fabric-covered shades lined in rose. One of the lamps was placed far from the bed, at the opposite end of the room, near the small sofa. I had all the lamps put on dimmers, so that the light could be easily modulated in the room. After making these changes, voila! Amour entered. Except for the lamps, the new, romantic feeling in this bedroom was created entirely with fabrics and color. None of the furniture was replaced. With only the backgrounds and bed coverings changed, their room was transformed and became their own romantic sensuous bedroom.

Dressing the sensuous bedroom calls for a command of all the senses. Color and lighting are crucial, as are the patterns and textures of fabrics. Your eyes and ears and fingertips, and even your senses of smell and taste, will be awakened in this sensuous environment.

Take a moment to visualize a sensuous bedroom. Here is a list of *Bedroom Words* that can be associated with how you might feel in this room.

- ❖ Desire
- ❖ Mystical union
- ❖ Sensitive Intimacy
- ❖ Fascination
- ❖ Charm
- ❖ Delight
- ❖ Enchantment
- ❖ Dreams
- ❖ Magical
- ❖ Fulfilled wishes

Contrast this against *Kitchen Words* that can be associated with thoughts of a kitchen:

- ❖ Crisp
- ❖ Efficient
- ❖ Warm
- ❖ Inviting
- ❖ Family and friend's gathering
- ❖ Gleaming surfaces
- ❖ Convenient
- ❖ Cozy

Do you see the difference?

Reread the bedroom words. What colors are you seeing? As you say the words are you seeing rich jewel tones? Are you seeing frothy sherbet color tones? Bedroom words such as, "mystical union, "sensitive intimacy," "enchantment," and "fulfilled wishes" evoke thoughts of shades and tints at both ends of the color spectrum—the deepest and the palest.

Visualize the colors you see when you read through the kitchen list. What colors do you picture when you say those words? Do you see vibrant colors? Gleaming stainless steel? Burnished copper tones? Or, as you read through this list, do you find yourself seeing colors in the medium tonal range?

As you do this mental exercise you'll find that, just as your response to different colors varies, so too, does your response to various shades of color. The mood you want to create is closely tied to the tones of color you choose

Of course, bedrooms that are smartly turned out in crisp Wedgwood blue and white, or bedrooms that are "frilly" can certainly be very pleasing. But these bedrooms are not sensuous.

The feminine partner in a relationship, will usually assume that the male will want the bedroom be a very comfortable room—preferring it to a sensuous bedroom. However, in most cases, she's never asked him. She assumes that after fifteen years of living with him and sleeping next to him, she knows what he wants his bedroom to be like.

And she probably does—as far as she's explored the subject. But it's probable that in all those years of living with him and sleeping next to him she's never asked him how he feels about a sensuous bedroom.

When I suggest it, she'll smile and say, "Oh, no, Sam would never go for that."

When I ask Sam, I get a different response.

"Sam, how do you feel about a sensuous bedroom?"

He smiles broadly. "Sensuous?" he asks with a smile. "Tell me more."

I have special, fond memories of one couple whose home I designed. He was seventy-eight and she was seventy-six. They had been childhood sweethearts. Yet, with all their verbal endearments they expressed to each other, and the obvious pleasure they had in each other, they maintained separate bedrooms, and both found this satisfactory. Her bedroom was really in many ways her refuge and her retreat. I thought that she would enjoy having this room, where she spent a great deal of time, be an extension of her charming, romantic self—as sensuously appealing as she was.

My client added a special insight. She explained that not only did she like having a room all her own, but she also felt that by maintaining separate bedrooms she had preserved the mystique in her marriage. Since this couple had been happily married for more than fifty years, I could only assume that her belief was valid. What's more I could see that it was definitely working for them!

I asked her to tell me how she would like her room to feel to her, and of course, how she wanted it to look. When I mentioned "sensuous," she looked surprised, but then responded candidly that, yes, she thought she would like such a room.

A few months after I finished her bedroom, I received a call from my special client. "Elaine," she began, "Of course, I knew that I would love my new bedroom. But I must tell you a secret. My husband loves it every bit as much as I do. He has coffee with me here every morning. We read the paper together and talk. And he loves spending the night with me and waking up in the morning in my sensuous bedroom."

Once again I was reminded that "sensuous" is a far more expressive word than "sexy." "Sexy" is marvelous for the heat of the moment; those surges of passion, but "sensuous" transcends all the seasons of our lives.

Sensuous, however, does not "just happen" in a bedroom. It must be invited in.

Invite Sensuous Into Your Bedroom

Many bedrooms can be turned into sensuous, very special places, with some fairly simple changes. The trick is to know *which changes to make.* Once you understand the principles of "sensuous," almost any bedroom, regardless of the style or period of the furnishings, can become a sensuous delight. I say "almost," because some styles cannot be adapted to sensuous. By its very nature, sensuous can't happen indiscriminately. It must be carefully and thoughtfully invited in.

Rest assured that a sensuous bedroom for a single person works just as well as a couple. I remember vividly when I first became an available single person after years of being married. My friends rallied around me, offering advice. One friend walked into my home and declared, "Elaine, there is absolutely no way a man will be interested in you for long." My gaze followed hers. I saw what I considered a warm and comfortable home.

"Where is your stereo?" she asked. "Music is vital for romance. And you need candles. You have no candles." She shook her head in pity and I knew she was thinking of all the solitary years that stretched before me.

After she left I remembered that I kept some candles in a kitchen drawer—in case of power failure. I got them out. They were bent.

When my daughter heard my story, she told me that a friend of hers had told her that no man could ever be interested in her for long because she didn't keep her refrigerator stocked with a variety of foods. In fact, her refrigerator usually didn't have more than a half empty container of cottage cheese, water, and a pint of milk that might or might not be turning.

I submit that there is more to 'sensuous' than food and music. What's more, not only is sensuous not fattening, you don't need a musical ear to appreciate it. If you're alone, or with someone you care about, sensuous always feels good. Married, unmarried, divorced, widowed, or whatever the personal circumstances of our lives are—everyone feels delighted and delightful in a sensuous bedroom. To create your own sensuous bedroom, read on.

Give Your Bed a Colorful Special Place

Because the bed is designed to be used when people are in horizontal positions, emphasizing the horizontal lines of the bed enhances the sensuous mood of any bedroom.

One of my favorite ways to define the bed's lines is also the easiest and most effective way: Fasten ½ inch molding to the ceiling around the bed. Then you're ready to *visually lower the ceiling above the bed* by covering the space directly above it with a solid-colored or patterned fabric, or wall covering. Whether solid, patterned fabric, or wallpaper, they should have your major or anchor color. A patterned fabric will probably include two or three of your accent colors as well. The fabric on the ceiling and/or the walls can be shirred or draped. Wall covering, of course, will be applied flat directly to the ceiling. Using this fool-the-eye method the ceiling will appear to be lowered By adding colorful interest to it, the ceiling covering more clearly defines the horizontal lines of the bed. A lowered, colorful area over the bed always emphasizes its intended intimacy.

Place Your Bed In an Alcove

If you're planning structural changes in your bedroom, an alcove setting is a wonderful way to give your bed a special place in your sensuous bedroom. Constructing a false ceiling just above where you plan to place your bed, means that you'll drop the ceiling 12 to 15 inches below the room's actual ceiling. This will easily give your bed a predominant and significant place in your sensuous bedroom. Walls on either side of the bed are necessary to complete the alcove. These walls can be only 18 inches deep and they'll suggest that a bed is set within an alcove. During the construction period you'll need to look elsewhere for your sensuous experience!

If you have a narrow room you can create an alcove feeling by using color and fabric. Place the long side of the bed against one of the narrow walls. Install short rods at the ceiling in front of the bed so that curtains suspended from the rods can hang straight down and then tied back. This will create a daybed effect. Use the same pattern and colors you're using for your window treatment, or introduce another accent color here. Paint the ceiling the same color as the walls. Or, draping the ceiling to create a tent-like feeling with the daybed fabric, is a beautiful way to treat the ceiling that will give the room not only a sensuous mood, but an unexpected dramatic feeling.

Solid-colored or patterned valances and canopies

These canopies give beds a special feeling and look. In a sensuous bedroom, the valance above and around the bed is traditionally shirred or gathered or draped, essentially following the body's rounded contours. A canopy must also have a soft look on the underside, and therefore, is often lined with a soft fabric.

A partial canopy

This can also provide a special setting for your bed. This type of canopy extends approximately thirty inches out from the wall over your bed. To plan this properly, lie down on the bed and note the location of your waist. Drop a mental line from the ceiling down to your waist. This is the distance where a partial canopy should extend to. Valances and canopies should repeat the colors you're using on your bed covering. Of course, you might also be using these colors in wall covering and/or window treatment.

Place your bed "On a Pedestal"

This is still another way to create a special atmosphere. A 4 inch deep platform for the bed can be and cover the platform with a soft-to-the-touch carpeting that has both depth and pile. Continue the carpeting throughout the rest of the room, or interrupt the continuity by using another color of the same or similar carpeting on the platform. This color can be the major, anchor, or accent color.

A hard-surfaced platform—in fact a hard surface floor throughout —has no place in a sensuous bedroom. In a sensuous bedroom, how your toes feel when they touch the floor is as important as water is to a cup of tea. Without water there can be no tea. Without a soft floor there can be no 'sensuous'. When your bare foot dangles off the bed, your toes need to feel soft warmth. Having a foot fetish isn't necessary to appreciate the tactile pleasures of bare toes touching soft textures. The softer and more deeply piled the carpeting, the more sensuous the sensation. Ideally, everything in a sensuous bedroom should be "wrapped in soft." In fact, if there's an operative word to describe a sensuous bedroom, "soft" is the word.

Brass beds, Victorian heavily carved bedsteads, contemporary styled beds, and beds of every period fit easily into a sensuous bedroom and lend themselves to bed coverings of every design and color; comforters, duvet covers, and deep, cushy pillows. Still, the bed alone cannot create the illusion of the sensuous bedroom.

A lowered ceiling, a canopy over the bed, a valance surrounding the bed, the bed on a platform—the bed given it's proper place, it's rightful domain and significance—only then will the mood be set for the deliciously sensuous new room.

Give the Walls Special Treatment

Fabric, especially in frothy tones or deep jewel tones, is my favorite way to introduce sensuality into a room. Later in this chapter I'll tell you about other colors, patterns and types of fabrics, but for now it's important to know that fabric whether applied directly to the wall, shirred or draped, immediately raises the romantic temperature in a sensuous bedroom.

Bronze mirror—a special mirror that diffuses and softens the lines of anything reflected in it—is another special way to treat the walls in a sensuous bedroom. In a sensuous bedroom, a mirrored wall is most effective when accompanied by a solid or patterned fabric on the adjoining walls so that the fabric is reflected in the mirror. In all cases mirror should be handled subtly. Of course, mirrors themselves are not intrinsically sensuous. It's how and where mirrors are placed in the bedroom that provides the mood—softly suggestive or blatantly sexy. We're definitely going the "softly suggestive" route; touches of mirror that will afford glimpses rather than full reflections. We want a sensuous, subtle feeling, and glimpses of us, regardless of the condition of our bodies, aren't merely provocative, they're also kind. Given the choice, who wouldn't prefer to be glimpsed in the nude, rather than fully scrutinized?

Create an Aura With Lighting

In a sensuous bedroom, lampshades are lined with pale pink or rose-colored fabric. The light through this fabric appears as a delicate blush, and bathes the complexion of the entire body in a lovely glow. Is your face less than perfect? Cellulite? Imperfections? What imperfections?? In this magical glow anything less than perfect fades into oblivion.

Because bedroom colors are at their best when the room softly glows, install dimmers or rheostats so that the lights can be lowered for special moments. We all know that some things are better left in shadow. And that sometimes it isn't necessary to see every detail of a person.

Banish the Bedspread

In a sensuous bedroom no one worries about wrinkling a spread. Bedspreads have no place here. Soft, plushy, down comforters in lighter-than-air colors or in rich jewel tones are practical as well as romantic. In a sensuous bedroom you don't have to first turn back the bedspread.

Soft and Inviting Floors

Tile and hardwood floors, no matter what color, have no place in a sensuous bedroom. Neither do throw rugs. Nobody wants to make love on a throw rug.

If You Like Your Bedroom Furniture, Keep It!

Almost any furniture will work in a sensuous bedroom. Wood furniture can be stripped of its finish and refinished with another stain. It can be painted or lacquered. Drawer pulls, handles, and hinges can be changed. Although there is no such thing as sensuous bedroom furniture, "sexy, romantic furniture" continues to be advertised. Suggestive bedroom furniture is too obvious, somewhat vulgar, and frankly embarrassing.

A Sofa For Two is a Must

Soft seating for two is important in a sensuous bedroom—a sofa and/or a large lounge chair. You'll find that your bedroom is the perfect place for it. Depending on the space you have available in your bedroom for one or both of these pieces, recover or slip cover them in the same fabric as you're using for your window treatment and/or bed covering. Or introduce a fabric in a solid color here. Recovered in the major or anchor color, your sofa and/or lounge chair can be a perfect addition to your room. These pieces will enable you to, in addition to your bed, have at least one other piece of furniture on which you can recline.

Place a table beside the sofa and/or lounge chair. Draped in either a solid-colored or patterned fabric, the table should be at the very least large enough to hold two glasses and a plate of food large enough for two to share. It's essential to have a table close to the sofa or lounge chair, because food is a special attraction in a sensuous bedroom. In this bedroom sensuous tastes are meant to be satisfied.

Place a small lamp at the opposite end of the room from the bed and use a rose-colored bulb in it. The lamp should have a low light setting, and can be located on a table, dresser, desk, or on any surface away from the bed. This light source supplements the bedside table lamps. It can be dimmed and left glowing when other lights are off. Although this is a mood light, it also has a practical purpose—because nothing spoils a mood faster than bumping into a piece of furniture in the dark. It's hard to feel sexy when you're in pain.

Some Colors are More Sensuous than Others

Black, when it's the background for a beautiful pattern, or when it's set against coral, apricot or peach, can be deliciously dramatic in a sensuous bedroom. However, almost any color, whipped to its most fragile, frothy tone, can produce a sensuous effect and stimulate the visual senses. The lightest lemon yellow, the most delicate powder blue, or the palest apple green, all can raise the level of desire. These are the provocative colors used by lingerie designers. In addition to black, the perennial seductive color, the sherbet tones of colors always entice.

Sensuous Colors List—Colors that feel at home in a sensuous bedroom
   ❖ Black
   ❖ White
   ❖ Any deep jewel tone of red, purple, blue, green, or turquoise
   ❖ Rose
   ❖ Apricot
   ❖ Peach
   ❖ Silver grey
   ❖ Coral
   ❖ Frothy, lighter-than-air tones of yellow, pink, lavender, blue, or green

How do you decide which colors to use? Start by asking yourself:

Does this color make me smile?

Does this color excite me?

Would I like to wrap myself in this color?

Would I describe this color as a soft color?

Would I describe this color as a hard color?

As you think about each of the colors you're considering, you'll find yourself quickly eliminating some, and feel yourself drawn to others. Bright colors are too sharp in tonal value to belong in a sensuous bedroom. Instead, choose frothy pale tints or deep jewel shades. For example, select a deep plum instead of a bright purple, or an emerald green instead of a darker hunter green. You can create an equally sensuous effect with deep jewel tones, as you can with the frothier tones. In the right tones almost any color can work well in your bedroom with one exception: BROWN. It's the single exception. Brown is a deadly color in a sensuous bedroom!

If you find a color you like, you may want to use it in more than one way. For example: Tone on tone is wonderfully sensuous. A pale rose-colored fabric, soft and billowy, with a deep, rose-colored pattern, will always be sensuous.

Let's do a fast color-check for your bedroom. Read through the list of suggested colors again.

Are any of the colors on the Sensuous Color List presently in your bedroom?

_____

Are you using any jewel tones or frothy tints?

_____

Are you using any tone on tone fabrics?

_____

Do you have any brown in your bedroom, aside from wood tones on furniture?

_____

Some Patterns Are More Sensuous Than Others

Almost any pattern, from abstract to floral, in almost any combination of colors, can work well if some basic guidelines are observed. The pattern must stir the senses. You should feel the desire to touch it There are some patterns that will never do this. Even in the most sensuous colors, plaids, geometrics, checks, and lattice designs do not belong in a sensuous bedroom. With this exception: If the pattern is *woven into the fabric* instead of *printed on it,* the effect can be different. Patterns woven into a fabric are often sensuous. Remember, the sensuous bedroom is a room where touching and feeling is eminently important. It's a room of feelings. I cannot overemphasize how important it is to be careful in your choice of pattern when planning this special bedroom. Floral patterns that conjure up thoughts of touch, and even scent, belong in a room where you want all the senses to come alive.

Some Fabrics Are More Sensuous Than Others

When selecting fabrics, you have a great variety from which to choose. Combine sensuous colors with sensuous fabrics and you cannot miss. Satins and velvets top the sensuous list. Soft velvets are wonderful in a bedroom, and satin, of course, is equally delightful, but not for its look alone. The way satin feels against the skin makes this fabric a sensuous favorite. Most of us are exceptionally sensitive to satin. Within the first few seconds of contact, the fabric takes on the temperature of the body. It then puts the body through additional change, cooling or warming the skin to the room temperature. This change is subtle, but exciting. Because we're all sentient beings, we're constantly aware of these subtle temperature changes. For this reason, satin is an excellent choice of fabric. For a deliciously sensuous look, select satin in shades of rose, apricot, or peach, marigold, coral or choose a silvery grey.

Linen, on the other hand, which also adjusts itself to the body's thermostat, should never be used in those areas of a sensuous bedroom where the fabric will come in contact with the body. Linen, even in the most sensuous color, doesn't have the soft texture necessary for this special, sensuous room. Unless linen is combined with cotton, it is stiff to the touch and too often an unexpected, scratchy fiber will move out of the weave. While some surprises are fine in a bedroom, sudden scratchy surprises are not. In this bedroom all fabrics must be soft to the touch, and wherever body touches fabric, the sensation must be caressing, soft, and deliciously pleasing.

Sensuous Fabrics List—Fabrics that feel at home in a sensuous bedroom.

- ❖ Velvet
- ❖ Satin
- ❖ Gauze
- ❖ Soft lace—so soft it drapes easily
- ❖ Chiffon
- ❖ Pongee
- ❖ Moire
- ❖ Taffeta
- ❖ Shantung
- ❖ Soft, polished cotton

How do you decide which fabrics to use? Start by asking yourself the following questions:

Does this fabric billow or flow?

_____

Is it extremely pleasant to the touch?

_____

If you're still not quite sure, take this simple fabric test. Close your eyes. Run your *fingertips and palm* over the fabric. Do this two or three times. ***Run your fingertips down past the second knuckle and then run your palm over the fabric.*** Keep your hand slightly cupped while you are doing this. As you raise your wrist and continue to feel the fabric, block any distracting thoughts from your mind. Keeping your eyes closed, stroke the fabric in this manner for a few moments and discover how this fabric feels.

There are two important fabric rules for a sensuous bedroom: Fabrics must look and feel soft to touch, not harsh or scratchy; and fabrics must have fluidity, not look or feel stiff or unmoving.

Jot down the fabrics you're presently using in your bedroom. Are these fabrics sensuous?

	Fabric	Sensuous?
Bed Covering		
Wall Treatment		
Window Treatment		
Floor Covering		
Chair or Sofa Covering		

Consider Sensuous Styles

Many decorating styles can be adapted to a sensuous bedroom. Sensuous transcends almost all periods and styles of furnishings. However, not every period and style can transcend to sensuous.

Early American bedrooms are delightfully virginal. They are crisply Puritan. They are not sensuous. Mexican colonial bedrooms are fresh and charming. They can be unique and whimsical. They are not sensuous.

Contemporary bedrooms bold geometric or checked patterns, can be fun, interesting, and invigorating. They are not sensuous.

Nor do obvious bordello-like touches belong in a sensuous bedroom. Mirrors on the ceiling are not sensuous. Their placement is obvious, vulgar, and they are very difficult to clean!

To help you picture the way this special room can come together, I'll describe what I call "Traditional Sensuous Bedroom" and following it other styles. Once you understand the basic rules that transform a room to sensuous, you'll find that you're able to turn almost any period and style into a sensuous bedroom.

Discover the Traditional Sensuous Bedroom

I received a call from a woman who told me that she was especially unhappy with her bedroom. Some years ago she had worked with an interior designer, but neither she nor her husband ever felt entirely comfortable in their bedroom.

When I met them the first impression I had was that they were both unusually tall people. They later told me that he was 6'6", and she was 6'1".

Their bedroom was furnished with elegant and expensive furnishings. But all the furniture and especially the fabric patterns, were completely out of scale for them. The designer had treated their king-size bed in a way that made it appear delicate and much too small as compared to their sizes.

As we spoke I had a strong hunch about them. I asked if they would like a sensuous bedroom and both immediately wanted to know more about this "style." I told them a little about the sensuous bedroom and they were very receptive and even enthusiastic. After we'd talked for a while I felt sure that they would be happy with a *traditional sensuous* bedroom, with all the furnishings scaled and proportioned to their size.

I gave them a quick course in traditional sensuous bedroom fabrics. I told them that fabrics in the sensuous bedroom are diaphanous, often transparent, and that velvets and chenilles are lovely when used on upholstered furniture in this room; and that in fact, all fabrics look and feel soft. There are low lights, perhaps some candlelight.

They both liked lacquered furniture—would this be appropriate in a sensuous bedroom? I told them that black lacquered, even pale lacquered furniture is lovely in a sensuous bedroom. Colors are often tones of peach, rose, silvery grey, coral, and all the luscious sherbet tones. They both loved the feel and look of satin. I told them that satin is lovely in a sensuous bedroom and that it would be beautiful in their bedroom—very likely on their bed and elsewhere as well.

There would be mirror somewhere near their bed, and their bed would have a special place. They told me that they liked the concept of their bed on a platform curtained with soft draperies at the corners. In addition, I suggested that they have another area in the room where they could have a sofa so that they could sit together, and because their room was large enough, they could have a lounge chair as well.

Their existing bedroom carpeting, thickly piled in a lovely tone of apricot was perfect. "In a traditional sensuous bedroom," I explained, "one color is dominant. The other colors are used as accents and the accent colors are easily picked up in accessories. Your apricot carpeting will very likely be the dominant color."

As I described the bedroom I envisioned for them, with soft lighting on a table next to the sofa in the sitting area, they listened as if they were being told a fairy tale. As we talked about this style of bedroom, I told them that the traditional sensuous bedroom originated in the 1930s—the Arte Deco period. It's a bedroom that Joan Crawford or Jean Harlow, movie stars of that period would have had. It has satin, lace, velvet, large, poufy pillows and at least one ottoman. When grey is used, it's often found in satins and velvets. This bedroom has thick carpeting and flowing draperies. There should be other furniture, in addition to the bed, which invites you to recline. Every surface the body touches must be soft and everything is designed for sinking into. My clients loved this idea for their bedroom, and ten years later they told me they still loved everything about their sensuous bedroom

Turn Almost Any Style Into Sensuous

Now that you've been introduced to the elements of a sensuous bedroom, you can decide upon the style you want for your bedroom—Traditional, French Romantic, French or English Country, Contemporary, Oriental, or any other style of sensuous bedroom. Color and fabric choice will determine the differences; the basic design directions remain the same.

Guidelines

❖ Choose fabrics that are soft to the touch and to the eye: fabrics that *look and feel* soft.

❖ No hard wood or tile floors—only soft carpeting.

❖ Use lamp lighting only. Overhead lighting is too harsh for a sensuous bedroom

❖ Give your bed very special place in your sensuous bedroom

❖ Have a loveseat, small sofa, a lounge chair, and a table large enough for two glasses and a plate of food you can share.

Traditional Sensuous

Quick Guideline:

❖ One color is dominant. This is the 1930s Arte Deco Period

❖ Black or pale colored lacquered furniture—even one or two pieces works beautifully

Colors
 ❖ Ivory
 ❖ Peach
 ❖ Rose
 ❖ Apricot
 ❖ Grey—in satins and velvets

Fabrics
 ❖ Satin
 ❖ Velvet
 ❖ Any soft, billowy fabric that shimmers

Patterns
 ❖ Go with solid colors. Forget all patterns

French Romantic Sensuous

Quick Guideline:

❖ No single color dominates. Colors are used together, appearing with spontaneous abandon. And lace has found its home in this lovely room.

Colors

❖ Ivory
❖ Pinks to rosy reds
❖ Leaf green
❖ Aqua
❖ Lavender
❖ Apricot
❖ Coral
❖ Peach
❖ Gold tones

Fabrics

❖ Damask
❖ Faille
❖ Soft velvet
❖ Soft lace
❖ Brocade

Pattern

❖ Tone on tone patterned designs—patterns that are *woven into* the fabric (not *printed on* the fabric)

This room has a delicious, languid feeling. Draperies puddle onto the floor. Colors range from medium tones to deep pastels to pastel tints. A profusion of pillows, some covered with a soft lace, some only trimmed with soft lace. Certainly satin belongs here. The bed can be partially canopied and/or raised on a platform. The sofa can be upholstered in velvet or any of the soft fabrics you choose—even a soft faille would be lovely here. While no single color dominates, every color adds to the romantic atmosphere of this bedroom.

Country French Sensuous

Quick Guideline

❖ Pattern is as important as color in this room. Toile-de-Jouy (often known as Toile, the French country scenes printed on cotton) and floral patterns—small, medium, or large—are very desirable here; ivory or deep, rich jewel-tone backgrounds. Allow yourself to use colors with ease and know that your room will love it and you'll love looking at it and living in it.

Colors

❖ Deep violet
❖ Jade and deeper greens
❖ Amethyst
❖ Sapphire
❖ Jet
❖ Yellow
❖ Reds
❖ Deep pink

Fabrics

❖ Soft cotton
❖ Deeply piled velvet

Pattern

❖ Floral—pattern in any size
❖ Toile—pattern in any size

This room is a veritable garden, where you can picture yourself lying in a field of blooming flowers. Iris, peonies, periwinkle, violets—flowers abound. The toile pattern that depicts country life is so charming you'd leave home for it, except that you're already home! This is an intriguing, provocative room that exudes exuberance. The bed could have a full or partial canopy; the chair and/or sofa upholstered in velvet or in the same pattern—toile or floral. Both, bed and sofa are heaped with patterned pillows. The draperies are full and heavily gathered, and if you have a yen ruffles, they're very much at home here; on bed covering, draperies, dust ruffle, and pillows. The combination of velvets and soft cottons, used together in this room further impart a delightful, spontaneous and romantic feeling.

Contemporary Sensuous

Quick Guideline

❖ Solid colors are the best choice for fabrics and wall treatment. This is a sensuous bedroom. Therefore, there are no geometric patterns here! Use *brass, chrome metallic finishes only as accent* textures/colors.

Colors

❖ Black
❖ Grey
❖ Peach
❖ Rose
❖ Apricot
❖ Any frothy pastel shade
❖ Ivory

Fabrics

❖ Any soft fabric **EXCEPT LEATHER**
❖ Satin
❖ Velvet
❖ Chenille

Patterns

❖ Only patterns that are woven into the fabric. No printed patterns.

The contemporary sensuous bedroom is sleek. There's a controlled headiness to the room, a subdued and exciting feeling here.

The draperies hang straight. The bed is placed on a colorful platform; the bed covering is soft and downy. The quilting pattern on your comforter could have a wavy design, rather than a box quilt or a traditional quilting pattern. Satin and velvet pillows on the bed, sofa, and/or lounge chair. This is a room for people who feels at home in an understated environment—yet they want warm and cozy.

Oriental Sensuous

Quick Guideline

❖ Oriental, Country French, and French Romantic use almost the same colors and fabrics. Here, the oriental inspired furniture style will also determine the differences.

Colors

❖ Apricot
❖ Dragon's blood red
❖ Peach
❖ Yellow
❖ Coral
❖ Black
❖ Jewel tones of every color

Fabrics

❖ Brocade
❖ Damask
❖ Faille
❖ Velvet

Pattern:

❖ Tone on tone—pattern **woven into** the fabric
❖ Floral patterns

An Oriental sensuous room emits a soft luster. Nothing shines here; everything has a *subdued sheen.* This room evokes a certain feeling of mystique. The bed is at its most beautiful when it is curtained with draperies at all four corners. Straight hanging draperies are at the windows. Deep jewel tones can be used for all the backgrounds in this room. This is a room where black could be the anchor color or the major color because rich jewel colors such as emerald, ruby, turquoise, and yellows are fabulously exciting against black. Fabrics are rich and lustrous. Furniture, whether finished in a black or brown stain, or with inlaid or lacquered designs, enhance the lovely Oriental mood of this sensuous bedroom.

Secret Garden Sensuous

Quick Guideline

This is a nostalgic, romantic room. The bed looks delightful with gathered a dust ruffle of a gauzy fabric layered over the under duster of the major fabric used in the room. Use painted or wicker furniture in this room to create a fresh, secret-garden ambience. No pale blue here. Pastel blue gives this room a little girl look—the last effect you want.

Colors:
- ❖ Ivory or medium white creates the effect of walking onto a cloud
- ❖ Any two solid medium toned colors—except pastel blue

Fabrics:
- ❖ Eyelet embroidery (pre-washed to remove stiffness)
- ❖ Voile
- ❖ Gauze
- ❖ Chintz—the softer kind—or if that's not possible, use the traditional stiffer chintz in small ways; a pillow, a seat cushion, as the trim on your bedside table skirt.
- ❖ Soft, polished cotton

Pattern:
- ❖ Use solid colors here; no patterns

This is a place of pristine whimsy. There's a feeling of generosity, open heartedness, about this room. The bed appears surrounded by infinite yards of fabric. It is canopied or curtained, and soft eyelet embroidery appears on the bed covering and on the draperies at the windows. These draperies are full, wide panels and may be caught by wide tiebacks of the same fabric. The furniture in this room can be white or a color in a tint—a light tone. Wicker is at home in here as well, with the inside back, seat, and arms upholstered.

All-white is sensational here; this is the room of a turn-of-the-19th century romantic heroine.

Victorian Sensuous

Quick Guideline

This is one of the most sensuous bedrooms you can create. Deep red is a must here. So is velvet. An intricately carved wooden bed would be the piece de resistance in this room.

When planning this room, select two major colors. One of the easiest ways to do this is to let yourself be guided by the most dominant colors in the patterned fabric you decide to use in this room. In other words, look for the fabric first. Choose a pattern that contains deep shades of the colors you love in jewel tones. If you can't decide which two colors to extract from your patterned fabric, follow the steps outlined in the Color Maven chapter. Buy a half-yard of a solid-colored fabric you like, tack it to the wall in your bedroom and place it on your bed, so that you'll be viewing it vertically and horizontally. You'll soon now if it's right for you. Choose two major colors and then use these colors and choose two accent colors. You'll find your accent colors in the patterned fabric, or you may prefer to bring in two other contrasting shades or tints.

Colors:

❖ Deep red
❖ Black
❖ A combination of any jewel tones

Fabrics:

❖ Velvet
❖ Brocade
❖ Heavy satin
❖ Damask

Patterns:

❖ Tone on tone—the pattern *woven into* the fabric
❖ Contrasting solid colors—always in deep jewel tones
❖ Striped
❖ Floral—always in deep jewel tones

This room has an opulent and ardent quality about it. Velvet, in any and every rich tone of red, appears at least twice and often more, in the room. The colors create a passionate feeling. Fabrics are luxurious and tufted upholstery is seen on at least one chair or sofa; a familiar style with its broad, rounded, and tufted arms and inside back. The carved bed in a Victorian sensuous bedroom is usually a gorgeous focal point in this room. The bed covering is in jewel tones of velvet, damask or heavy satin. Furnishings in this room are in deeper tones, and antique accessories are at home in this elegant environment.

****

To turn your room into a sensuous bedroom, decide which look you prefer. Re-read the guidelines, colors, fabrics, and patterns provided for that style.

List your sensuous bedroom colors:

If your style calls for one dominant color, note your major, your anchor, and your accent colors.

_____

_____

List your fabrics:

Include your existing fabrics if they fit with your new style.

_____

_____

List your patterns:

Describe those patterns already in your bedroom if you plan to keep them.

_____

_____

List your wall treatment:

Do you plan to include any mirror on your bedroom walls? If so, where?

_____

_____

Note the color of fabric, wall covering, and paint you're planning for your sensuous bedroom.

_____

_____

_____

List your floor treatments:

Does your existing carpeting work with the sensuous image?

_____

What color is it?

_____

Is it thickly piled?

_____

Carpeting is an expensive item, so if it's the proper texture, keep it and work with it, even if it isn't in one of your favorite sensuous colors. You don't need to design your room around the color of the carpeting. Instead, make it one of the accent colors in your room. However, if your carpeting has a geometric pattern, or the texture is flat or coarse, it will be difficult for you to create a sensuous look in this room. In this case, you may wish to purchase 3 or 4 yards of a solid-colored, thickly piled carpeting in one of your new sensuous tones, and place this carpet at the foot of your bed. The addition of a large, soft expanse of colorful carpeting will draw attention away from your present flooring material. Remember: If it gives a soft appearance and feels soft, almost any solid-color carpeting can work. If you're planning to change your carpeting, note your new color.

_____

List your window treatments:

Will the pattern, fabric, and color of your present draperies or window covering fit the sensuous style you're planning for your bedroom?

_____

Can you make simple changes that will create a sensuous look—for example, by adding a valance, rope-and-tasseled tiebacks, soft sheer under-draperies?

_____

Use this space to think through any contemplated changes.

_____

List your bed treatments:

Is your bed now given a special place in your room?

_____

How can you give it a more distinctive place in your bedroom?

_____

What is the design of the bed you're planning?

_____

Are you planning a platform for the bed?

_____

Will you use draperies at the four corners of the bed?

_____

Will you use draperies only at the head of the bed?

_____

A canopy?_____

A partial canopy?_____

List your lighting treatments:

Note the styles, and locations of lighting in your bedroom.

_____

Will the lampshades be lined with a rose-colored fabric?

_____

Are you adding additional lighting?

_____

Will you add dimmers?_____

List your bedroom furniture treatments:

What pieces of furniture do you plan to keep?

_____

Which ones do you plan to replace?

_____

What pieces do you hope to add?

_____

Are you planning to recover or slip cover a sofa and/or chair you presently have?

_____

Does your existing furniture—chest of drawers, dresser, headboard or any furniture need to be altered in any way to enhance the style you're creating?

_____

If so, how?_____

_____

List your accessory treatments:

What colors are the lamp bases, pillows, and vases? Your accessories can be in any of the colors you are using in the room. Or, you may bring in new accent colors. List the colors:

_____

_____

All the answers you record on these pages will enable you to create a sensuous bedroom that will give you enormous pleasure.

Make Sensuous Decisions

If you decide to transform your bedroom into a sensuous bedroom, remember that the colors, fabrics, and patterns you choose will help determine the style of your new bedroom. Although every style listed in Color Your Life is sensuous, each creates a distinctive mood for a room.

By following the guidelines and answering the questions in this chapter you'll find that you've embarked on a deeply fulfilling design project that will give you enormous pleasure—in the doing, and in the completed beautiful sensuous bedroom you've created. The payoff? You'll find that your sensuous bedroom speaks to you as no other room in your house does, or can.

To Note What You Want to Remember

Chapter Eight
Suddenly Single

If you wake up the morning after your partner-in-life has asked for a divorce, or has left the relationship you both had, and the reality hits you: "I am alone," you're suddenly single.

If you wake up the morning after you've buried your partner-in-life, and the reality hits you, "I am alone," you're suddenly single.

At first you concentrate on getting through each day, on finishing a conversation without filling up with tears, on having a meal and caring about what you're eating. And then one day—at least a few weeks for some, a few months for others—you suddenly feel an overwhelming desire to change things in your home. You need to have your home look and feel like who you are now, who you've become, at this time of your life. You feel the need to nest again and you intuitively recognize that your home is where *you emotionally live*. And that it is in every way your refuge.

As you accept your altered situation, your home becomes your focus. If you decide to remain in the home that you once shared with your partner, you might look around and realize that although it's been feeling so much without life—without energy to you, and without love, now is the time for you to make some important changes to your home. This is the place where the two of you dreamed, and planned, and lived together, and now you're about to make it a home for only one. You have memories you're finding hard to shake.

If you move out of your home to a new place, you have different problems to face. If you've taken your bed, a favorite chair, a sofa, a table, and a lamp, as you try to arrange your furnishings so that the place looks like it's beginning to feel like home, you discover that where once your furniture fit into your old life, it now looks strange and alone in these new rooms. In a very real sense, your suddenly single's home looks like you feel: Out of place and drained of energy.

In both instances, introducing color into your life at this time can play a vital role in speeding up the healing process. Color is a restorative element. Not only is it therapeutic, color also enables you, the Suddenly Single, to indulge yourself in an unexpected and delightful way. Surrounded by the colors that make you happy, wrapped in the hues that bring you joy, as you color your life, your emotional scars begin to heal.

How to Put Color Back Into Your Life

To understand the role color can play at this time of your life, read through the following list of questions and answer each question honestly. Have you been feeling a deep desire to:

❖ Return to a happier time in your life

❖ Assert yourself

❖ Be cared about by someone who cares about you

❖ Blend some of the good of your old life into your new life

❖ Become the person you want to be—in a way reinvent yourself

❖ Simply be happy

❖ Feel that you belong instead of feeling disconnected

❖ Have a place that is your private space and refuge—especially if your children are living at home

❖ Have a balanced life

❖ Be indulged

❖ Laugh and have fun

Most people will answer yes to some of these questions, but as a Suddenly Single person, you will answer yes to almost every question because your answers express what you yearn for.

At first, happiness seems impossible. But as you heal, you realize that you desperately need to put joy back into your life; that you need to laugh again, to feel enthusiastic about life, and you very much need to feel good about yourself. Here is where color in your life steps in and becomes the restorative element in your healing. Because we all have a natural relationship with color, this element has a profound effect upon our emotional healing.

My research has shown that for healing to begin, the suddenly single person needs to begin with the room that is now completely yours—your bedroom, where very likely you spend most of your private time. More than any other room in your home, your bedroom will be your sanctuary, and immediately upon entering it, should provide you with a deep sense of comfort and security. To help you evolve so that you're restored and rejuvenated is the sole reason why now is the time for your bedroom to become the refuge you require. You want to more than just survive. You want to thrive!

As your healing continues, you'll want to make changes in other rooms as well. However, don't pressure yourself to do more than you're deriving pleasure doing. Enjoy the doing. Be gentle with yourself. Go slowly and follow your natural instincts with whatever you're considering changing. Colors at this time are a crucial element to your emotional recovery. So listen to, and follow your instincts as though they are words you're hearing. *Listen to your instincts.* The best way to begin this phase of the healing process is to be guided by the following steps:

Look at the Colors In Your Bedroom
How would you describe the mood of this room?

_____

When you walk into your bedroom do you feel relieved to be there?

_____

Or is it still too full of sad memories?

_____

When you're in bed and look around, are the colors relaxing to you?

_____

Do they make you feel uneasy?

_____

Would you say that you love the colors in your bedroom?

During this period when you're dealing with loss in your life you'll find that you respond positively to certain colors and color combinations. I call them "Restorative Colors." Yellow, turquoise, coral, and deep jewel tones of any color bring with them much needed and remarkable feelings of optimism. Why these particular colors and tones? I honestly don't know.

When I ask my Suddenly Single clients how they feel about yellow, I usually hear that the color reminds them of sunshine. Regardless of their personal association with this color, yellow is a positive mood-booster at this fragile time of life. Teamed with accents of coral and/or white, this combination unfailingly lifts the spirit of a Suddenly Single person. Yet, as you know from having taken the Supermarket Test and seen your results, whatever colors you love are those that will lift your spirits and to which you'll respond with an optimistic and enthusiastic view of life. This is what color does. It's the most natural and most benign miracle worker!

Blue, used as a major, anchor, or accent color, is another particularly healing color. I've wondered about why this is so, and believe that because bluee is a universal color—the color of the sea and sky—people who find themselves Suddenly Single find it to be a soothing color. My research has also shown that newly alone people are drawn to, and find comfort in the depth and richness of jewel tones.

Although I normally don't separate colors for men and colors for women, when working with a Suddenly Single client I do make a distinction about the color gray. Suddenly Single men are affected differently by gray than are women. Men respond positively to gray. Women don't. Suddenly Single women's association with this color can best be described as 'gray'—or dismal.

Contrasting this affect of gray bedrooms on women, at this time in their lives, men will find all tones of gray restorative. Suddenly Single men will often consider having a predominantly gray color scheme. Using the Color Bars, this is easily accomplished. Choose any three tones of gray on the Even or the Odd Side of the Color Bars and you'll be sure that these grays will match beautifully with each other. Use these grays on the walls, floors, the backgrounds—walls, carpeting, and draperies—your duvet cover, sofa and/or a lounge chair. The various tones of gray blended together in a single room create a bedroom men love being in. Team the grays with solid black table bases and clear and black glass tabletops. Use ivory-white for all the lamp bases and ivory-white or black for the lampshades. This room becomes a very masculine sensuous bedroom for a suddenly single man.

Use Your Color Memory

Suddenly Singles have a marvelous tool in their color memories. As you discovered earlier in this book, each of us carries memories imprinted within us. For the newly single adult, these memories can become a lifeline. To rediscover happy colors, as a Suddenly Single ask yourself what colors you remember when recalling a particularly happy time in your life. Think about a joyful and carefree summer vacation or a favorite childhood activity. A woman might recall the color of a dress she wore to the senior prom when she was certain she was in love forever.

Answers often reveal colors never before considered. When I asked one of my Suddenly Single male clients to describe the colors of a happy time in his life, he told me that the Supermarket Test brought to light for him that his favorite colors are brown and green—the color of earth and the color of grass. They triggered color memories for him, and he remembered that as a small boy he was happiest when he was pushing his toy trucks on the ground outside his home, and as a grown man he still loves those colors. Today his bedroom reflects his recollections. The walls are lacquered grass green and the major colors in his bedroom's fabrics are shades of camel—his "dirt."

If you're emerging from an unhappy marriage, recall those times in your life or those experiences that *you did not* share with your former spouse. As you sort through your past to discover happy colors, remember that the colors you come up with are only for you, to help you launch your new life.

Color Memory List

Let's regroup for a moment. The first step in designing your new bedroom is to assess your present room.

- ❖ Identify the colors presently in your bedroom.

- ❖ Ask yourself whether any of the colors from your color memory are restorative (uplifting) color combinations.

- ❖ Check the present color scheme in your room against your color memory to see if any of the colors have positive past associations for you.

It's very important to know the colors that make you smile. So, if you have not yet taken the Supermarket Test, now's the time to do it!

Use Color to Affect Your Emotional Changes

As you read through your Color Memory list, you might have three or four, possibly five colors you've written down. Compare them to the Supermarket Test colors you discovered are the colors you love. If they're similar or the same, you're normal, just like everyone else. Why? Because we all respond today as adults, to the colors we intuitively and instinctively loved when we were very little. Once we get our minds out of our way, and stop analyzing if a color goes with another color—and we simply respond to the beauty before us as children do—our colors present themselves to us, for us to love them. Which is what the Supermarket Test is all about, and does for us when we allow it to work for us.

Now is the time to decide which of these colors to use in your new bedroom and how you want to use them. Before you make your choices, explore all your possibilities. You'll discover, as you consider all the ways to use and combine color, that color alone, and in various combinations, has a remarkable effect on you right now. At this difficult time in your life you are especially sensitive to color. You may find yourself responding to tones of colors you never even noticed before. Don't make hasty decisions. Take your time and consider all your options before selecting colors for your new bedroom.

Remember, too, that this is a perfect opportunity for you to assert yourself with color. Try offbeat color combinations. If red is on your list, team it with orange. If you love purple, how about amethyst, (another tone of purple), and orange, or purple and pink? Have a fling with colors you may never have considered combining before and you'll find that, even if you've always stayed with conservative choices, at this time of your life, what you might term a "crazy" color combination, you're loving and lifts your spirits.

Deep, rich colors are also exciting to you now. If you want to display a collection of objects you have a special fondness for, deep-colored walls will show them off to their best advantage. Ceramic, bronze, porcelain, terra cotta, brass, and chrome—all are beautiful against richly colored walls. Oriental rugs take on an especially important look in such a room. When you're using deep tones on your walls, plan to use the medium values of the other colors in your room for bed covering, floor covering, or upholstery. Here is where the Color Bars will help you enormously with so that you'll be able to immediately see how deep jewel tones, medium tones and light tones look together. The work has already been done for you with every color matched and coordinated to the other colors. Because the colors are already matched, you can be sure that you won't make a mistake when you're combining colors.

Contrasting colors have a soothing effect on Suddenly Singles. To create this atmosphere, choose any deep tone of color that appeals to you as your major color, then accent this deep shade with two or three brighter tones of colors. Be conscious of contrast when selecting fabrics for the bedroom. If you choose a deep shade as the background for your fabric, select a pattern that has brighter colors against that deep color. Using colors in this way—brighter tones of colors against deeper tones of colors—creates an uplifting mood to any room.

Or, you might consider using color to incorporate some of your old life into your new life. Suddenly Single people who know the colors they love may want to have certain colors they lived with before the unhappy condition they now live with came upon them. They had a favorite color then, and they might want to have it in their homes again at this time of their lives.

One of my clients knew that she loved blue. For thirty-three years, she and her husband shared a bedroom that was predominately blue. Eight months after the reality of her suddenly single condition hit her, she decided to make real changes in her life and her home.

When we met at her home it was apparent to me that she was particularly fond of the color in what had been their bedroom, and was now her own, and I told her that I believed that eliminating blue from her room wouldn't bring her the restorative qualities she was seeking. The fact was that she loved blue. So why do without what she loved? I suggested that instead, she keep the blue she loved, and use it only in fewer ways, not as the dominant or major color, but as one of her accent colors.

We used a new major color, a medium tone of rose, a color she told me she'd ways loved, and white in her accessories—lamp bases, lampshades, and in the background color on the patterned upholstery fabric where blue was a secondary color in the pattern. The blue became a bright accessory color in her new room, along with a dash of deep green (number 1 green in the Color Bars). By using color in this way, she was able to have the blue that represented a happier time in her life, yet still move forward with new colors in her present life.

Color can help you establish a bright, new identity. This is the time to dust off your unrealized aspirations and desires and make them become realities in your life. Begin your search by exploring the possibilities of color in your life. If you want to bring a dramatic quality and feeling into your room, introduce this mood with black. Choose a fabric with a black background and a deep jewel toned floral pattern printed on the black background. Use this fabric abundantly in your bedroom: On your bed covering, draperies, pillows, and if it pleases you so much that you want more of it in your bedroom, upholster your sofa and/or lounge chair with it.

A good recipe for recovery is that if you love it, use it. If you love it, it's good for you. What's good for you is giving you pleasure. And because more creates more—use more of what gives you pleasure.

Don't be timid or tentative when you're selecting the colors you'll be living with. You'll soon find that your road to coloring your life is being paved with both the deeper and higher tones of the colors you love. They will lift your consciousness.

Colors we love, and the tones of the colors we have around us do this to us. It's another intense example—a beautiful indicator of the natural relationship every one of us has with color. It's nothing new that came upon us when we were teenagers and we became acutely aware of color—it's what we instinctively responded to when we were infants and for the first time we saw and reached for the colorful object before us.

Color speaks to us in a language all its own, and when we hear it we react to it with our hearts.

Try Some Practical Tips

Whatever colors you choose, if you plan to have painted surfaces in your room, consider a low sheen enamel or lacquer rather than flat paint. Lacquered walls in eggplant purple or rich burgundy could provide a beautiful, dramatic background for your new life.

Because a Suddenly Single person will often feel confined in small spaces, consider using color to make a small bedroom appear larger. To make small appear spacious, contrary to what you've probably read—that white makes a room look larger—avoid using a white background and instead use a medium tint (a lighter tone) of your favorite color. Use this color on the walls, as the color of your carpeting, and on shutters or blinds at the windows.

If you're feeling that you'd like to do something whimsical things with color, the following are some examples to follow or to inspire you with a few of your own:

❖ If you're using a red-and-yellow color scheme and have a bookcase in your bedroom, paint the outside of the bookcase sunny yellow and the inside deep tomato red. Or visa versa.

❖ If you're planning to use a rich eggplant color in your bedroom, paint your old bedroom dresser the same eggplant color. Add new brass hardware, and you'll have injected a spark of new life into your bedroom and your furniture.

❖ Give your treasured antiques a facelift: Combine them with delightfully surprising choices of fabrics and colors. Say goodbye to predictable colors and fabrics. Instead of velvet, upholster elegant chairs in bright candy striped corduroy. Instead of brocade, upholster an old sofa in red-and-white stripes of awning canvas or a multi-colored cotton plaid.

❖ Paint a wood-framed chair one of your favorite new colors and choose cotton or linen in a floral or check as upholstery. Second-hand store chairs work wonderfully for this treatment.

❖ Treat yourself to a brightly colored telephone for your bathroom so that you're connected to the outside world at all times. The colored phone is not only a delightful touch of luxury, it also assures that you won't miss out on anything important. Again and again, my Suddenly Single clients tell me that this simple tip works wonders for their spirits, not to mention their social lives. A bathroom phone is that important!

How To Get Started

Now let's get down to work. You've assessed your current colors and decided which colors to keep and which new colors to add. You also have an idea of the mood you want to have in your home—soothing, exciting, whimsical, dramatic—or to reflect your own self, a combination of moods. The new you is now ready to emerge. You've decided on your major and accent colors, and if needed, an anchor color. Now, what do you do? How do you translate this color plan into a well designed, emotionally satisfying environment?

NOTE: It's normal and usual for Suddenly Single people at this time of their recovery to find that they're lacking confidence in themselves.

Experiment With Color

Begin by matching paints, fabrics, and materials to your color plan. If you're not working with an interior designer, many of whom will bring fabrics to you in your home, plan to scout fabric shops and paint stores to see what is available.

We all know that the light in each room varies between the day and evening hours. When you follow the RULE to test all colors of paints, all wallpaper, and all fabrics in the room you're considering them for, you'll be viewing these materials under a variety of lighting conditions.

Always ask for the largest available fabric samples so that you can see as much of the color and/or pattern as possible. By viewing paints, wall coverings, and fabrics in various lighting conditions, you'll eliminate unpleasant surprises, and when you find that you've made the choices you love, your self-confidence will soar.

Begin with your backgrounds. Decide which surfaces you can change and which ones you would like to change. Very likely, you'll find it easier and less expensive to change the color of the walls and window treatment than to change the floor covering. So although you might *like to change* your floor covering, due to your budget constraints, you *can change* the color of your walls and window treatment.

Let's begin with the walls. If you've selected a deep shade for your major color, you have a couple of options. You can paint two adjacent walls a deep shade, and paint the other two walls a lighter tone of that same color. Or you may want to go with a more dramatic approach, and paint all four walls the same deep shade. Either wall treatment will give your room balance.

RULE: Always paint or paper at least two walls the same color. Never paint or paper one wall a color different from the other three, because the single wall painted in a different color than rest of the walls in the room, stops the eye and throws the room off balance. *Always paint or paper two adjacent walls the same color.* This is a rule that should always be observed. However, it's especially important that newly single people observe it because, at this time of their recovery, they're in great need of balance in their lives. Follow this "Two Walls" rule regardless of the wall treatment you're planning. If you decide not to paper all four walls, but to also have painted walls, paper *two adjacent walls,* and paint the other *two adjacent walls.*

Let's suppose your present bedroom has white walls and ceiling, beige carpeting, a pale green duvet cover or bedspread, and draperies in a brown, beige, and green geometric pattern. And your budget doesn't allow you to make all the changes you want to at this time.

By using paint you can affect an important change in your room. Paint the *walls and the ceiling* of your bedroom *the same color*—mango and apricot are compatible with pale green (your bedcover)—and will give your bedroom an instant lift. Or of course, paint your room in another color of your choice. However, the ceiling and the walls should have the same color. When your budget allows you to, change the geometric pattern in your draperies by treating your windows to a new look; draperies in a soft pattern that bring in colors compatible with the walls, or in a solid fabric in a deeper tone of the color of your walls. You'll find your colors are already combined for you in the Color Bars.

Replace your pale green bedspread with a down comforter and comforter cover in your new drapery fabric. On your bed, mass pillows in a variety of shapes and sizes, some covered in the same fabric you're using at the windows that appears in the draperies and duvet cover, and to further repeat this fabric, you might recover the seat of a small chair in the same drapery fabric.

In this example, you've transformed your room by introducing a new color, and eliminating brown. In effect, your bedroom has a new look—and what's easily as important, it feels newer and better and more like who you are now.

Be Good to Yourself

Whatever your financial situation, Suddenly Single people do best in their recovery when they're living with the highest possible quality in their environments. Be good to yourself. You'll feel better for it. If you need to purchase a new bed or dresser, buy the best quality furniture you can afford. If necessary, do with less, but buy the best, which translates to your living with the best. Explore all your purchasing possibilities now—store sales, personal connections (is your mother's friend's son-in-law in the furniture business?), estate and garage sales.

Indulge yourself. Now is your time to make decisions that make *you* happy. If you love a purple-and-orange color scheme and a friend tries to talk you out of it, assert your taste. You no longer have to answer to anyone. Now is *your time* to color your life to please yourself.

Confident with your choices, excited by all your colorful possibilities, have fun with your bedroom. If you're coming out of an especially difficult time, leave your old colors behind. Make a list of the colors you've used in your previous bedrooms, and then resolve not to use any of them in your new retreat. Don't look back because you're now creating new memories!

Expand Your Horizons

After you've made the changes in your bedroom and you're considering making changes in other areas of your home, you'll definitely benefit by keeping your color perspective and choosing those colors you love—those colors you've never before given serious thought to having in your home. For example: If you love tangerine and green but think that teaming these colors with beige or white would be safer—forget the safe beige or white! Instead choose either tangerine or green for your major or anchor color, and white for your accent color. Your room will instantly be very personally your own—reflecting your personal color preferences.

Combine patterns. Geometrics and floral patterns are very successful pattern combinations and are often used together in the living, dining, and family rooms. Unlike having a geometric pattern in your bedroom, in the living, dining, or family room, this geometric pattern works very well.

To create and keep a balanced feeling and mood in these rooms, it's important to be aware of the scale of the two patterns you're using. If one pattern is small, the other should be larger. Also, at least two of your personal colors should appear in both patterns.

Do you like the look of plaids and prints in a room? I can see why you do. They make for a happy combination. How about a striped fabric in the room? Used on a chair seat, or as the trim or welting on a large floral patterned pillow for your sofa? Very nice look! Expect that combining geometric and floral patterns will bring an exciting new look you'll love—most especially at this time of your Suddenly Single recovery.

Many of my clients have been amazed at the effect color has on them during this painful period of their lives. Indulging in surrounding yourself with color helps restore an important sense of self. It's a visible and silent means of support. It enables single people to make positive statements about who they are, what they like, and how they feel.

Putting color back into their lives, they've told me, enables them to reaffirm themselves. Color in your life and confidence in yourself go hand in hand.

Introducing colors into a Suddenly Single person's environment can have dramatic consequences. Initially upon meeting him, one of my clients appeared to me to be a quiet, dignified, and somewhat intense man. In my studio and in his apartment he was serious and low-key. Then, a few weeks later, I was astounded when I saw him at an art gallery opening. Surrounded by clear, vivid color, the true man emerged. *This* gentleman was personable where my client had been reserved. *This* man was witty where the other had been serious. Surrounded by radiant colors, *this* man smiled openly and laughed easily. His beige surroundings, I realized, were acting as a sedative to his personality. I knew at that moment that my intuitive decision to put color into his home environment was right on target.

Color did wonders for this very nice man. His beige sofa was reupholstered in rich burgundy. His drab olive green wing chair now wore a navy blue, burgundy, and green plaid fabric. These pieces of furniture, with a comfortable armchair, tables, and a handsome desk, sat on a navy blue geometric-patterned rug that had yellow and burgundy in it. The entire effect was dashing and masculine. A couple of weeks later he told me how much he was enjoying his apartment, and that he was certain that the *color*, not the furniture, made the difference. "I needed these colors much more than I knew," he added.

I agreed with his assessment, because color has always been a safe haven for me. When everything else in my life was turned topsy-turvy, the color in my home always provided an emotional safety valve for me that I knew I could depend upon. Again and again I hear from clients who have found their own true colors. They tell me how adding this one vital ingredient to their lives made a dramatic difference for them.

Try Sleeping On It!

Many of my Suddenly Single clients use color to rediscover themselves. One friend of mine knew she was finally healing from an unhappy marriage when she found herself feeling enthusiastic about doing her new apartment. "I feel that I'm just now discovering who I am. I'm learning to respect myself in a way I never did before, and I realize that I definitely want my home to reflect the new me."

As we discussed her plans, we talked about the colors she would enjoy living with. I suggested pale jade green for her living room walls, but she disagreed. "I think I would feel better with white walls," she replied. I recognized that after nine years of living with a domineering partner, her natural love of color had been squelched. Her husband had insisted on "sophisticated" brown-and-beige throughout their contemporary home, and although she was now divorced, she felt safer with white. White is the absence of color.

I reminded her that a few years ago she told me that she loved florals and chintzes and soft tones of almost every color. She smiled, but was unconvinced. So I suggested she take a color test, what I call the Sleep Test. The results would be helpful to both of us, I explained.

"Tonight, just before you drop off to sleep, say to yourself: *'I command my subconscious mind to reveal to my conscious mind the colors I am happiest living with.'* Then go to sleep. When you awaken you'll realize that your subconscious mind followed the command of your conscious mind exactly as you instructed it to. You'll know that the answer is remarkably accurate, and that you've been shown your true colors—the colors you really love."

The next morning she telephoned me early. "I couldn't wait to tell you what happened. First of all, I actually had a good night's sleep last night, for the first time in months. And the colors I saw…" She described yellows, greens, and a purple iris color that she had visualized in her dreams—all the colors she loved. I did her living room walls in a beautiful leafy green, and we brought her favorite mellow yellow into her bedroom. There is no doubt in her mind that her colors helped her to regain her identity and feel confident about herself. Color therapy is not a myth. It works with us because of our natural relationship to color.

The Sleep Test is the best way I know for a Suddenly Single person to reach out for color. Most people enjoy taking this test, and discover that their subconscious minds clearly tell their conscious minds those colors they'll be happiest living with. There's no mystery about why the Sleep Test works. Call it the power of suggestion, or self-hypnosis, the fact is this: The human mind is a wealth of untapped energy. Once we instruct our subconscious minds to reveal colors to us, we see vivid splashes of color in our "working dreams."

The Sleep Test is simple and effective. I'm often told that just before my clients awaken they see an especially strong streak of color and they awaken knowing the colors they'll choose to live with.

Some people, at this time of their lives, naturally know the colors they want to have in their homes. Freed from an unhappy situation, they assert themselves immediately and rejoice in their new independence. Yet, I always advise them to take the Supermarket Test because this Test, very often shows them that colors which hadn't appealed to them previously, are now colors they see themselves using as accents or even as a major color in their homes.

Other Suddenly Singles are completely at a loss when it comes to color preference. For them I strongly recommend putting their subconscious mind to work as soon as they feel the desire to change their environment. In addition, I suggest that all Suddenly Singles retake this test in six months or a year, when the healing process has progressed. It's surprising to see the subtle color changes the subconscious reveals.

Remember to always speak to your subconscious mind *in the present*. Ask it to reveal the colors *"I am"* happiest living with. Don't ask your subconscious mind to predict the future. It can only tell you what is going on at the present time within your subconscious mind.

When you decide to take this test, record your feelings and the colors you see. Be sure to use the exact wording: *"I command my unconscious mind to reveal to my conscious mind the colors I am happiest living with."*

Record the date and record the colors you "saw."

Now, make your choices and get ready to have some fun using these colors in your new bedroom, and eventually, throughout your home.

Go Forward With Color In Your Life

Although color is not a total panacea, it does offer a significant avenue for a Suddenly Single person to take toward recovery. It's a soothing, healing natural element. Applied liberally at home, color can help to heal the wounds inflicted by a divorce or death.

We know that it's difficult to construct a timetable for the healing process—we're all so different and each of us has had different experiences. Yet, you can be sure that your urge to change your home environment comes over you at about the same time that you make it to the middle of the bed after years of sleeping on your own side. At that moment you know that you're going forward.

Making it to the middle of the bed signifies that you are ready. This silent signal at this point is a clear indicator that this is the time to tap into your subconscious, take the sleep test, and bring new color into your new life.

To Note What You Want to Remember

Chapter Nine

Life After Throw Pillows

Most people run out of decorating and design ideas after they've hung art on the walls, placed throw pillows on their sofa, and positioned another green plant in their living room near their favorite chair. However, once you know some color secrets, you can work magic in your home. You can make large rooms feel cozy and small ones appear larger. You can add depth, perspective, and drama to your environment. You can wrap up a room with fabric, or light up your life with candlelight. You can create deliciously colorful focal points that will add vibrancy and interest to any room in your house. Best of all, you can imbue your home with the flavor of your own personality, and transform ordinary, boxy rooms to become the fresh, original and personalized environment that projects a particular and distinctive person—You!

Dress Up Those Bare Bones

For all kinds of reasons, too many of today's homes are built with little more than bare bones personality. Too many homes are without the gracious, high ceilings in homes of the past. Gone, too, are the beautifully carved moldings that dressed these homes. Today, unless your home cost a million dollars or more it's likely that you'll find it to be devoid of gracious decorative details. Instead, what is available and what you inevitably buy are homes that are waiting for the architectural elements to rescue them—to lift them from what they really are—unfortunately uninspired, ordinary living spaces. Try as we might to fill them in with furniture, window treatments, and such accessories as plants and paintings, we often end up with, although not identical, somewhat similar cookie-cutter homes.

There really is no authentic substitute for the subtle detail of yesterday's graceful carved moldings. But, hand-carved moldings are extremely expensive today—and fine craftmanship is not easy to come by. However, there is another way to create this mood of elegance: the same detailing found in moldings of past centuries is now reproduced with high-density polyurethane foam. These synthetic moldings are exact replicas made from molds of the finely carved originals. They lend themselves beautifully to color and come alive when they're painted. So much so, that often experts are fooled.

Example: Paint wall or ceiling moldings white when you're using a deep or jewel-tone color on your walls. For a traditional, classic feeling, use Wedgwood-blue walls with white moldings.

Example: Reverse the color scheme on the doors by painting the doors white, and the door moldings the same deep or jewel tone you are using on your walls.

Example: If your walls are white or a light color, contrast the moldings with paint matching the anchor color you are using in the room.

Use color and moldings to turn a plain front door into an inviting, exciting entrance. Moldings are easily applied to your door with small nails. Choose any color you like for the door and paint it with an enamel paint, which resists fading. The color selected for the door does not have to appear anywhere else in the exterior or interior of your home. If you choose a vibrant shade, such as red, yellow, or green, arrange the molding in a simple, pleasing design, perhaps an oval or a rectangle, and paint the molding shiny black or bright white.

Imagine welcoming your family and friends with a leaf green door trimmed with bright white molding or a marigold yellow front door accented with a black door design you created with relatively inexpensive moldings. Your colorful front door will send out positive thoughts to everyone who enters.

Available where building construction materials are sold, synthetic moldings come in a variety of patterns, styles and sizes, from ornately carved to simple, Greek-inspired designs. (Dental molding derives its name from the fact that the geometric pattern closely resembles teeth.) The use of painted, colorful moldings is an economical way to dress up a wall, ceiling, or door. Moldings add a timeless feeling to any room, immediately enhancing it in a special, beautiful way. Moldings serve to create order and richness in any room in your home.

Give Colorful Ceilings Wonderful Feelings

Regardless of the size of your room, if you're using a deep tone of a color on your walls and prefer a light-colored ceiling, reach for the lightest tint of that color and use that on your ceiling.

To dress up any room with white walls, extract the dominant color from a fabric you are using in the room and use that color on the ceiling. Your major or anchor color will always be a good ceiling choice.

For a more dramatic effect in a large (i.e., 18x25 feet) room with jewel-tone walls, continue that same deep jewel shade on the ceiling. Add moldings painted in a creamy or white tint. A rich tone of color on the ceiling serves to create a more intimate mood than does a white ceiling in the same room.

For another effect, use a colorful wallpaper or fabric on your ceiling. To complete the desired effect, the same pattern should appear on at least two adjacent walls, as well as on the ceiling. If you decide not to use this pattern in the entire room, it is a good idea to use the ceiling pattern on the window wall and an adjoining wall only. Many papers have matching fabrics and you can use them successfully to repeat the pattern in your window treatment.

Patterned walls and ceilings work beautifully in powder rooms, kitchens, and bedrooms. The combination of color and pattern creates a feeling of warmth, intimacy, and charm. However, this look can become contrived when it goes into the public rooms in your home—family room, living room, and dining room. Think twice before putting colorful pattern on the ceiling in these rooms.

Let There Be Elegant Light

Moldings will particularly enhance your dining room hanging fixture. Encircle the fixture base with painted moldings positioned in a pattern on the ceiling, approximately six to eight inches from the hanging fixture. Choose this molding in a floral or leaf design. You may paint it the color of the ceiling or choose a contrasting color from the wallpaper in the room. Or you may want to match this ceiling molding to the color you are using on other moldings in the room.

EXAMPLE: if your walls are white and the wall moldings are bright yellow, you may want to paint your ceiling bright yellow and use white molding around the hanging fixture. By defining the area above the hanging fixture, you will give it added importance, focusing attention upon it and creating an elegant chandelier out of an ordinary suspended light fixture.

TIP: Add even more color-interest to your room by sewing, or having made, a fabric sleeve to hide the chain links that support the hanging fixture. The sleeve can be in any color or fabric you like, but it should be long enough so that the fabric gathers gently, and wide and loose enough so that it lies in soft folds.

Choose the fabric color for the sleeve from your major or anchor or accent colors. Almost any fabric will do for this sleeve, but do not use the major fabric in the room for the sleeve. Use an accessory fabric or introduce a new fabric here.

In other words, if your dining room chairs are upholstered in a medium-green faille fabric, have the sleeve fashioned out of velvet or moiré in another color appearing in your room. Cottons and velvets lend themselves well to this sleeve treatment To complete this look, repeat the sleeve fabric somewhere else in the room, perhaps on a pillow or a chair seat cushion.

Create a Beamed Ceiling

Think color when you see beams. Colorful beams are a wonderful addition to a room. Repeat the room's major color on your beams, or use the anchor color if your ceiling is painted a lighter tone. To retain a classic look with a white or light-colored ceiling, choose the deepest shade of the colors you are using else-where in the room, and use this color on your beams. This will probably be your major, anchor or accent color. To add whimsy to a light-colored ceiling, paint your beams a bright, vibrant shade. Borrow a bright color you enjoy from a pat-tern you are using in the room and carry it through onto the beams.

Reverse the scheme for rooms with deep-colored ceilings by painting your beams a light-to-medium tint. You may use a light tint of the ceiling color, or the major color in your room if it is a light tint, or your may lighten any of your anchor or accent colors by selecting medium-to-light tints. With a very deep or jewel-toned ceiling, select a pale tint of that color for the beams.

Synthetic beams provide great color opportunities. As much as I enjoy fine woods and wonderfully intricate carvings, I also appreciate the gifts that modern science has brought us. Not only are synthetic beams easy to apply to ceilings, they are extremely realistic in appearance. And let's face it. Unless you're entertaining a pro basketball team, who can see the beams that closely? Since these beams come in a variety of depths and widths, they can work beautifully in rooms of any size.

TIP: When deciding to add beams, remember this quick rule of thumb: Beams should be spaced at least two feet six inches apart in average-sized rooms; that is, in rooms that are approximately fifteen by seventeen feet. Beams are suitable and relevant in rooms with high ceilings, but they are equally effective when used in rooms of average ceiling height—seven feet six inches. I've successfully used beams with six inch depths (the distance from the bottom of the beam to the ceiling) and five inch width all the way to ten inch depth and six inch width in rooms of average ceiling height.

Make a Statement With Columns

Columns can also bring color into a room. Egyptians, Greeks, Romans, and architects of the Old South all appreciated the beauty of stately columns. If you think of columns as only white, look again. Synthetic columns can be painted any solid color in your room. They could be the major, anchor, or any accent tone you're using. Or they can be faux-painted to resemble beautifully veined natural color marble and even malachite.

This faux-painting process should be professionally painted. Be aware that this is an expensive process; however, the effect can be magnificent. Columns at the entrance to a living room or positioned in a room to define the space between rooms, bring a regal and elegant tone to even an ordinary interior space. The rich greens and blacks of faux-malachite or any beautifully veined faux-marble columns can be repeated again on moldings by creamy ivory walls.

When you take advantage of the vertical space in your room (the area above your eye level), you'll find that columns will visually extend your room because they draw attention to this unused space

By fooling-the-eye with the addition of columns that add to the illusion of greater vertical height, the brain believes this room has larger dimensions. Yet, in reality, the room may be of only average size. When you bring color and columns into your room, the most ordinary space in your home will be transformed to memorable in the most positive sense.

Wrap Up a Room!

Colorful patterned fabric is another way to add design interest to a room. Regardless of the size of the room, you are certain to add drama if you choose a pattern that has a deep shade or jewel tone as the dominant color. To create the effect of depth and perspective wrap the entire room—including baseboards and door frames in a patterned fabric you love. Multi-colored paisleys are superb here, as are small document prints—French, American, or English designs.

Madras bedspreads, printed with exotic, colorful designs, also make beautiful wall covering. Have the bedspreads paper backed first so that they can be easily applied to the wall. Your interior designer or fabric store can have this done for you. These spreads come in gorgeous colors and patterns and when they are acrylic-backed, the loosely woven madras becomes durable enough to use as a light-weight upholstery fabric.

To achieve a professionally wrapped effect, use matching fabric on the ceilings and on the walls. Often the fabric will contain most of the colors you will use in the room. Select a color from the pattern as your major color and use that in the window treatment, on the floors, and for important pieces of furniture.

A patterned cotton is a good choice when you want to wrap a room with color. Stay away from loosely woven fabrics, however, unless you have them reinforced with a backing.

Size—either of the pattern or the room—doesn't matter here. What matters is that the room feels swathed in colorful patterned fabric. This is the luxurious appearance you are after.

Just Hanging Around

Paint the walls of a boy's room with one of his favorite deep or bright colors. An enamel or lacquer paint is always smashing. Set off the vibrant color by hanging shiny hubcaps on his walls. His favorite color, combined with the interesting designs and sparkles of the hubcaps, will give his room more zest and panache.

Display hubcaps from cars of the forties, fifties, or sixties and use them almost anywhere on the walls in the room. Hubcaps are relatively inexpensive and wonderfully decorative. Prowl auto junk yards to start a collection. No matter where or how you use hubcaps—over a bed or desk, or simply placed at random on the walls—they look terrific. And for suggesting them, your son will think you're terrific, too!

Go from Cold to Hot

Do you have a bathroom that leaves you cold? Many bathrooms are small and functional, and also completely devoid of any personality. I've found nothing as effective in a small bathroom as a liberal dose of pure, exciting color. Whatever your design scheme, take a tip from Mother Nature and start with the "sky," or ceiling, first. Use a color on it that makes you smile, and from there your color scheme will naturally follow.

TIP: Paint the bathroom ceiling the blue of the most beautiful blue sky you can remember. Paint the walls a sunny yellow. Use shutters at the windows in whitest white and hang a shower curtain in a bright springlike print that repeat the blue, yellow and white.

Small Is Also Beautiful

Do you have a small room with which you've struggled, trying to make it appear larger? Let me guess. Did you paint it white? And were you disappointed because what you got instead was a small white room?

Before you close the door, push out the wall, or give up, try this: Turn what you considered a liability into an asset. Don't disguise the size of the room; celebrate the space you have. Select a colorful large-patterned fabric, and wrap the walls in this fabric—remembering to include the door frames and baseboards. Forget solid colors for this room. A large pattern in a small room, contrary to what you have heard, emphasizes the charm of the small space.

The mood in a room is determined by the colors and patterns used in that room. This is especially true when you're using a large-sized pattern. First decide on the mood you want to create, and then choose your colors and patterns accordingly. A large pattern that has a black or deep shade as a background will add drama. The same large pattern with a light background color will send out a different message entirely. A large floral, for instance, printed in jewel-tones against a black or deep blue background, will create an interesting mystique in your small room. That same floral, done in paler tints against a light colored background, will seem springlike, crisp, and cheerful—another stunning effect.

Use a patterned fabric or wall covering on the ceiling in a small bedroom or other private room such as a study. One continuous color or pattern on the walls and the ceiling in a small room creates a harmonious look. If your patterned wallpaper has a matching fabric use it to upholster at least one major seating unit; either a sofa, lounge chair, or large ottoman. You'll be delighted with the results.

For an alternate feeling, choose a pale tint of one of the dominant colors in the pattern and use that on the ceiling. Unless white is a dominant color in your pattern, don't paint your ceiling white. One continuous color in a small room creates a cohesive look. Repeat the wall covering pattern on at least one major seating unit, either a sofa, lounge chair, or ottoman. You'll be delighted with the results.

Tie Some On

Use a patterned fabric or wall covering on the ceiling in a small bedroom or other private room such as a study. One continuous color or pattern on the walls and the ceiling in a small room creates a harmonious look. If your patterned wallpaper has a matching fabric use it to upholster at least one major seating unit, either a sofa, lounge chair, or ottoman. You'll be delighted with the results.

The color of the ribbon should always be determined by the major, anchor, or accent colors you are using in the room. For example, if your draperies are a light-toned major color, select ribbon in the anchor color you are using in that room. If the draperies are in one of your accent colors, trim them with ribbon in your major or anchor color.

If you are trimming patterned pillows, borrow one of the deep or vibrant colors from the pattern and use that shade for the ribbon trim. If your bed covering is in a light-toned major color, dress up the spread or comforter with ribbon in your anchor color. Large pillows and bed coverings may lend themselves to the use of two ribbons of contrasting colors. You can lay ribbon on top of ribbon, creating patterns in wide and narrow bands of contrasting color. Let your imagination soar when creating ribbon designs.

TIP: As explained in *How to be a Color Maven*, you can trim draperies which traverse your windows by running one- or two-inch ribbon from behind the first pleat, down the drapery vertically and across the top of the hem.

TIP: Trim a bedspread or duvet cover by outlining the edges (where it touches the edge of the mattress) with one- or two-inch grosgrain ribbon in a contrasting color. You can repeat the grosgrain ribbon as a border along the bottom of the spread where it touches the floor.

TIP: Glue ribbon to vertical and horizontal wall surfaces that have been covered in fabric. Ribbon creates a colorful border around a room and gives it a uniquely finished look.

Join the Fine Art League

Introduce "fine art" into your home inexpensively. Buy four-color museum posters and frame them as you would a fine lithograph. Have the framer cut from the poster any printed date or description of a museum show. Posters take on new vitality when framed with colored mats. Select one of the poster's colors for the mat, and then have the poster finished in a simple frame. When a poster is treated in this way—matted and framed, it immediately moves subtly from the poster category into the "fine print" league.

To add importance to your new print, place it on an easel. Easels used in interior environments are instant attention-getters. Choose a gold-toned silver metal easel, or paint a wooden one in any of the accent colors you're using in your room. People are always drawn to art displayed on an elegant easel. Position your framed print in a special area of the room and spotlight it on its easel. You will have created an art illusion to be proud of.

See Stars In Black and White

Black and white are colors too! Welcome glamour into your home by hanging over-sized, six-foot posters of the movie stars of the thirties, forties, fifties, and sixties. Who can resist when Clark Gable or Marilyn Monroe beckons? Use these posters in your bedrooms or your family room, or on a wall at the end of a hall. These posters are visually exciting and everyone loves to become reacquainted with movie stars of the past. If you want to further accent the posters, have them museum-mounted with colored mats. This method uses a sheet of clear plastic mounted on cardboard, and is perfect for displaying poster art.

Set the Stage for Sculpture

If you own sculpture, it requires a special setting, and nothing sets off sculpture like color. Unfortunately, sculpture is often placed on a pedestal against a window or a light-colored wall. When possible, position sculpture against a deep-colored wall to enhance the work.

Texture also enriches sculpture. Combining color and texture behind sculpture gives the illusion of depth and perspective. To set off a single piece of sculpture on a pedestal, position it in front of a large plant, such as a tall banana tree. The color and texture of the leaves behind the sculpture create an interesting setting for the artwork, even if the wall behind is white or a light color.

If the sculpture is large, show it off. If possible, place it in the center of your foyer or entrance hall. The sculpture will become more important if the background against which it is set is a tone of the major color you're using in the room. To use your foyer as a gallery, select a medium tone of the color you want to use and cover at least two of the walls in that area with this color. Create an important space for your prize piece of art by choosing darker rather than lighter tints of color.

TIP: Treat the space around your sculpture as part of the work of art itself. Always light it, either from above or from the floor. Floor spotlights are available in handsome, unobtrusive designs that will blend with any decor. These floor spots are designed especially to light sculpture or large indoor plants.

Serve It Under Glass

Frame for effect! When a colorful rug does is hung on a rod, it doesn't become a "hanging." It remains a rug hanging on a wall. But if you mount that vibrant rug and frame it under glass, it becomes an instant treasure. Just as pheasant under glass is infinitely more appealing than a drumstick on a plate, a rug or quilt or fabric takes on added importance when it is framed in this manner.

Discover Neutral No-Color Knockouts

Once you've added color, you can afford a few neutral knockouts. One of the most inexpensive and effective ways to add interest and drama to a room is with an arrangement of bare twigs placed in a large vase. Bare twigs create a natural architectural element when set against a richly colored wall. Make certain you light the arrangement. Floor spots are excellent here.

Another knockout can be created with that old standby, a galvanized wash tub. Buy one in the hardware store and paint the outside of the tub any color you wish, as long as it is compatible with the room you are placing it in. Black or deep forest green work beautifully. Fill the tub with a mixture of black and natural-colored pebbles and plant a cactus garden in it. Top it with a circular slab of glass, four inches larger in diameter than the tub, and place another plant on this glass top. You will be pleased to find that the cactus grows well inside this new planter and requires watering only a few times a year.

Create Alcoves and Angles

Install shutters on the inside of a window frame to achieve a charming and original window treatment. You will need at least two panels hinged together so that they will angle out from the window. Ready-made shutters work perfectly here. Paint the shutters a color that contrasts with the walls. White is always a good choice, but you may extract any of the colors you are using in that room with delightful results. Light, bright, medium, or deep colors work equally well. Do not feel bound to use your major or anchor color for the shutters. This is a good opportunity to repeat a lesser-used accent color.

Add glass shelves to span the window. Arrange a collection of colored and clear glass objects on these shelves, interspersed with pieces of porcelain, such as plates, teacups, or tea pots. Any objects that are enhanced by light look wonderful in a window alcove.

Not only is this window treatment charming, it is also practical. The window shelves, now functioning as a curio cabinet or semi-etagere, do not take up any added floor space. This an excellent window treatment for a small room.

Walk Softly and Put Color Under Your Feet

Today's colorfully patterned commercial carpets offer a wonderful alternative to more usual floor coverings. I often use commercial carpeting for home kitchens. Not only are the colors and patterns good looking, but because it is dense and resists crushing and matting, commercial broadloom prevents soil from lodging beneath the surface. This makes the kitchen a warm and safe place for families with small children. An added bonus is reduced noise level, since carpet helps absorb sound. You'll find, too, that commercial carpets are easily cleaned. If your kitchen is small and the walls are filled with cabinets, look down. A carpeted floor—in a solid shade or interesting pattern—might be just the way for you to add needed color to that room.

Meet Versatile Mattress Ticking

Mattress ticking is a marvelous fabric to use on walls, upholstery, and draperies. No fabric is as underestimated as mattress ticking. Remember: it was initially developed to take wear and tear—bodies tossing and turning, children jumping on and off beds. The proof of the strength of this fabric can be seen in any old, sagging mattress—the springs may have sprung, but the ticking is almost always as good as new.

Mattress ticking is an excellent upholstery fabric. When paper-backed, mattress ticking will add elegance, inexpensively, to any wall in your home.

Elegant shades and draperies can be made from mattress ticking. Use it for Roman shades, with draperies of the same fabric, in your study, your dining room, or your teenagers' rooms. It even makes beautiful living room draperies.

Use grosgrain ribbon in a contrasting color—choose from your major, anchor, or accent colors—to conceal the construction tapes of the Roman shades. Rather than see the white tape when light comes through the fabric, disguise it with ribbon. Repeat the contrasting colored ribbon on the drapery, vertically down the closure and across the hem of the panels. You will love your new, elegant window treatment.

Best of all, this workhorse fabric comes in many colors. Treat mattress ticking as you would your favorite basic-black dress. You can dress it up or down and enjoy it everywhere in your home.

TIP: Mattress ticking looks especially charming in kitchens. Accent it with hanging utensils and copper pots.

Stitch Chic Sheets

Dollar for dollar, sheets are the best value when purchasing solid-colored fabric. The sheet manufacturers have been telling us this for years. And they are right. Sheets are the finest quality fabric. They come in a wide variety of colors, and they are woven to take a lot of wear. Upholster a sofa and a pair of lounge chairs for your sitting room with cotton sheets. Paper backed, they can be used on walls. Lined, they make luxurious draperies. To achieve an especially glamorous effect, hang the draperies high, up near the ceiling, and let them drape and puddle or bunch on the floor in the seemingly careless old French manner. Catch them back with decorative ropes that have heavy tassels.

TIP: Stay clear of patterned sheets. Because of heavy advertising, these patterns are easily recognizable. While the strength and dyes and quality of patterned sheets is just as good as that of solid-colored sheets, no one wants to hear, "How clever you are! You upholstered your sofa in sheets."

Advance Front and Center

We all agree, I'm sure, that centerpieces create charming focal points for dinner parties. They add your own special loving touch to your table. My favorite centerpiece is created from fresh fruits and vegetables.

Use a platter or flat woven placemat (anything without sides which will define a space on your table) and begin by placing two deep-colored, burnished eggplants on the platter—one at either end. Put a pineapple in the center of the platter and begin to heap fruits and vegetables onto this arrangement. I use a bunch of carrots, three or four turnips, at least three grapefruit, four or five tomatoes, and several oranges when I build this centerpiece. Keep heaping the fresh fruits and vegetables—making sure that the arrangement stays below the eye level of the shortest person at your table.

Finally, place some of the largest lemons you can find into the arrangement. (Because of the similarity in color and texture and tone, separate the grapefruit from the lemons.) Now surround your centerpiece with fresh leaves, and tuck some fresh blooming vines or flowers into the leaves. If this sounds like too much, it isn't. It is gorgeous, and, once you've tried it, you will realize how easy it is to control the height as well as the depth and width of the centerpiece.

Another lovely table arrangement is achieved by surrounding a favorite bowl with fresh leaves. Tuck figurines or small vases in among the leaves. Inexpensive objects look important in this special environment. Place votive candles in small glasses among the leaves to complete this special effect. You'll find that seashells collected from your last trip to the beach are suddenly transformed into what they really are—natural sculpture—when they appear among the leaves of your centerpiece.

TIP: If you happen to be taking the Supermarket Test, plan a dinner party. You now have fruits and vegetables on hand with which to begin building your centerpiece. You're halfway there already!

Light Up Your Life

Instead of using standard candles in standard candle holders, light your dining room table with votive candles. Clear and colored juice size glasses make excellent holders for votive candles. A white candle, glowing in a small colored glass at each place, will create a lovely feeling of intimacy around your dinner table and because these candles are low they won't flicker in your guest's eyes.

A charming chandelier can be created with candles. Suspend glass candle-holders at various heights above your table. To do this, use the special holders that look like teardrops. Available at candle shops these holders are designed for votive candles, and are made so that they can be easily suspended with "invisible" nylon thread. With votive candles on the table, these unique chandeliers lit by candles that appear to float in the air, provide a lovely and dramatic way to light your dining room table.

Group Your Group

To make the most of your favorite collectibles, group them. A colorful grouping should consist of objects that are approximately the same in size and proportion. The items in your grouping need not repeat the colors in your room and therefore, regardless of the colors of your collected articles they will always work.

Should you choose to assemble a monochromatic grouping of, for example—pewter, brass, or porcelain vases and boxes, again colors and textures in the grouping don't need to appear elsewhere in the room. The repetition of the textures and colors within the collection gives it cohesiveness and importance.

TIP: When selecting these items, keep their height approximately the same or within two to three inches of one another.

TIP: When arranging only a few items, a good rule of thumb to remember is that odd numbers are better than even. In other words, using three, five, or seven objects is preferable to using two, four, or six objects together. Beyond six, the number of objects in the grouping doesn't matter. Use as many as you wish. Accent your arrangement by placing a slightly taller piece in the center of the group, or by elevating one of the objects on a stand. By following this simple rule, you can turn any collection into a never-fail attention getter.

Build Up Instead of Out

Stretch the space in a small room by building a colorful platform at one end of the room—spanning the space from one wall to the opposite wall. The platform should be approximately four inches high and a minimum of five feet deep. Paint or paper the walls and ceiling in that area of the room a medium-to-deep color. The platform itself and the color within the space will help define the area.

You can cover the platform in the same color you are using on the floor in the rest of the room or in a contrasting color. The platform color can either match or contrast with the walls. Set off in this way, the platform becomes an instant study or sitting area. The raised floor surface will build in a feeling of larger space. You will create the impression of an extra room in what was a small, predictable space. Colorful platforms surrounded by colorful walls are another fool-the-eye, fool-proof design element.

TIP: If your children are sharing a room, use this platform idea to divide their room. Children love it!

Move It to Use It

Regardless of whether you're using a light, deep or bright color on your walls, you can define space easily by placing a piece of furniture at right angles to a colored wall, leaving the rest of the furniture placed more conventionally around the room. If you need to define an eating area, place the table at right angles to the wall. A sitting area? Use the sofa in this same way. When you arrange a piece of furniture in this manner, you'll bring immediate additional interest and dimension to your room.

Count On First Impressions

Awnings create a terrific first impression. They add glamour to a simple Cape Cod cottage or distinction to the plainest ranch house. Restaurants and hotels have always understood the impact of an elegantly tailored awning extending from the building. The addition of an awning to a place of business signifies that it is a dignified, special destination.

Why not send this same message out over your home front? In addition, an awning is a marvelous way to give vibrant color to the exterior of your home. Awnings are available in a dazzling array of colors and they adapt well to all styles of home design. They add architectural value to your home and, thanks to today's acrylic fabrics, which minimize fading, once an awning is installed, you can expect years of shade, pleasure, and elegance.

TIP: To add still more excitement to your entrance, use tied-back draperies at either end of the awning that extends over your front door. Trim your draperies down the closure and across the top of the hem with a contrasting fabric approximately two or three inches wide. Trim the "drop" of the awning as well in the same contrasting fabric. White is always a good choice of color for the trim.

Create a Room Within a Room

Use color and pattern to add a feeling of extra space to a plain room by installing a valance at the ceiling approximately and at least 6 feet from the wall at the furthest end of a room. You'll have created a 6-foot deep room and the width of this new "room" will be determined by the width of the actual room.

The valance can be in a solid color or in a patterned fabric. It can be the dominant fabric you're using in the room or you might introduce a second fabric here.

If your actual room is 15' by 17', your new "room" will be 6' x 17' nd the remainder of the space will give you a room that is 9' x 17'. You now have a room within a room that you can treat as two rooms adjacent to each other. In a room of this kind you can, for example, treat the "room" you've just created as your bedroom—it will easily take a Queen size bed and bedside table, a chair and a dresser or armoire. And the remainder of this 9' x 17' room can become your sitting room, your office or your study.

To further give the illusion of another room hang narrow panels of draperies in matching fabric at either end of the valance. These draperies can be straight hanging panels or the can be tied back. Paint or paper the three walls of the new "room" you've created behind your valance and draperies.

****

As you can see, the possibilities for adding color and architectural interest to your life are limitless. This is the time for you to look around your home and identify the dull spots, those places that cry out for visual interest. Now is the time for you think about all the options that are available to you that will enrich your home

However, before you do anything, this is the time to decide on the look and the mood you want to achieve. Mentally flip through the ideas I've given you in some of the chapters such as Life After Throw Pillows and Myths, Truths, and Tips to help you solve your decorating dilemmas.

You may be delighted to find that wrapping the walls of a room with fabric or wall covering, adding a floor spotlight to dramatize your favorite sculpture, or painting the ceiling of your bathroom in your favorite color will create just the effect you want to achieve.

It's true that when you design your home with your heart—instead of your head you can transform any house or apartment to become your dream home.

To Note What You Want to Remember

Chapter Ten
You and Your Interior Designer

Color Your Life has shown you how to live with the wonderful world of color in your home.

You've learned how to discover your own true colors—those special colors that speak to you—that you instinctively react positively to—and that you know are the colors you'll love living with in your home. You now know why you've felt unable to decide on colors for your home, and you have a special test (the Supermarket Test) to discover the colors you love. Also:

❖ You've seen how to put your colors to work for you. You know that a simple tool, the Color Bars, have the colors you'll want to consider using in your home—already color matched and color coordinated for you. You'll feel confident that any of the colors you choose for your home will be beautiful alone or together.

❖ You have many cool design tips and a lot of practical advice you can use when designing your home.

❖ You've seen that color is the single most important element that will express your personality in your home.

❖ You've seen how color speaks to us in a language all its own.

❖ You've discovered how using your favorite colors can help you heal during times of stress.

❖ You now know how vital color is in a Sensuous Bedroom

❖ You now know that regardless of your style preferences you can have a Sensuous Bedroom

❖ You now know How to Create a Sensuous Bedroom for you and/or your partner.

❖ You've discovered how to work with your child so that he/she knows that their bedroom is personally their own, created by them.

You're now on your way to determining what you can do by yourself, and if and when you might need to enlist the expertise of a professional interior designer.

Certainly I know that many people have problems with the concept of using a designer for their home. If at this time you feel that you don't need a designer, as you continue to work on your home by yourself and confront some problems, you may change your mind and think about consulting with someone who is a professional interior designer.

Therefore, knowing what a designer can do for you will be beneficial to you so that you're able to make the best decisions about what you can expect from the designer and about selecting that person to work with.

The professional interior designer's background is in interior architecture and space planning. The designer knows the interior furnishings market and understands classic as well as current building materials and how they function.

A designer can act as your consultant only, giving you the advice you need to continue with your project by yourself. Or the designer will work with you at every phase until completion of your home providing important specific services.

The shift that lifts fashion from ready-made to couture, can be applied to your home with the services of a competent and creative designer. However, because each designer has a unique style, it's essential that you choose that person to work with whose ideas blend with yours and whose style you admire. And what's most essential is that you choose someone you like as a person.

Some of the services your interior designer can provide include:

Space Planning: Planning interiors in your home or business so that the traffic patterns and furnishings in each room give you maximum flexibility, efficiency, and beauty.

Workrooms: Engaging the services of drapery workrooms, upholsterers, wallpaper installers, painters, cabinetmakers, carpenters, and carpet installers. Each must meet the designer's exacting standards, to ultimately create the quality of excellence a professionally designed interior will give your home.

Sources: Designers have market sources that are not available to the public consumer. In addition, the designer visits major home furnishing and interior design markets at least twice a year to keep current with this continually changing field.

Expertise: Professional designers know how fabrics, materials, and furnishing look and wear. Therefore, when they suggest new and innovative ways of using these materials, these suggestions often are design techniques you haven't thought of.

Purchasing: A designer can save you time and money—and prevent you from making costly mistakes.

Supervision: By supervising the work of craftspeople, the designer makes certain that completed projects will measure up to your expectations—and often exceed them. Shoddy craftsmanship is not tolerated.

Working Plan: Planning your total project in stages, so that you can work from one priority area to the next as your time and budget allow. A working plan will often take into consideration your changing needs during the next several years.

Budget: Making the best use of your decorating dollars and give you a realistic picture of what it will cost to accomplish all your design objectives.

It's very important to know what to expect from the professional interior designer and also to know what the designer expects from you.

The belief that the designer is an intimidating person who sees himself/herself speaking down to the client with an inflated opinion of herself is an old myth that vanished with the depiction of the all-knowing physician. Designers, as are other professional people, want to cultivate good working relationships with their clients. They listen to their client's needs; guide their clients to make the best purchase and design decisions, always taking into consideration their design budget dollars.

And often friendships develop between client and designer, who both knew that they liked each other before they agreed to work together. As they work on their mutually creative project they spend a lot of time together, and often their business relationship takes on another shared aspect—they become friends. It's this friendship that is often the unforeseen dividend.

How Do You Find the Right Designer?

Before you sign a contract with anyone, take your time and do some groundwork. Think of people you know whose taste is similar to yours and who have engaged the services of a professional interior designer.

❖ Ask them what their experiences were with their designer?

❖ Did they find the designer easy to work with?

❖ Did they feel that their designer guided them by showing them fabrics, furniture, cabinet designs, space plans, and generally worked with them to achieve what they believe they couldn't have done had they worked on their home by themselves?

❖ And the most important question: Are they happy with the results? If their reply is that they enjoyed working with their designer and they love the results, then you'll want to know the name of the designer and how to get in touch with her/him.

Then revisit their homes to look at the finished projects more closely. And ask this very important question: *Did the designer they worked with supervise all the work done on their home through the installation phase?*

Before you make a final decision, look at details of workmanship in the draperies, flooring, paint, wall covering installation, cabinet designs, etc.. You'll learn a lot about the standards of a designer when you see the finished product he or she approved.

Many cities have home and garden magazines that publish the work of designers and publish their names. Clip and save pictures of rooms that appeal to you, and *make sure to note the designers' names on the photographs.* Designers do have individual styles. Soon, you'll have a reliable list of the professional designers in your area. Call the designers whose work appeals to you and ask to set up personal interviews.

Visit model homes in your area, paying attention to the interiors of the homes rather than to the floor plans of the models. The real estate agent in charge will be able to tell you who did the interiors. Be aware that the interior designer may have been working with strict budget limitations in some cases, so rather than focus your attention on the specific furnishings you see in the model, look for appealing ideas and the mood created by the designer.

Pay special attention to the offices you visit—your doctor, your dentist's, your banker's. Most designers who do commercial work also plan residences. If you're impressed with the mood or style of an office, ask who designed it. Most people are delighted to be complimented on their surroundings and to be asked about the interior design and will be happy to give you the name of the interior designer. And, if you ask the all-important question *"How was she to work with?"*—they'll tell you.

If you find a special charity event where professional interior designers design the various rooms in a house, make time for a visit to see these houses. These events are often known as Show Houses. Be sure to take notes on specific design ideas.

When you find yourself in an interior environment that feels good to you, always feel free to ask who the designer is. After a while, you'll discover that you've accumulated an impressive referral list of interior designers.

All this time you're educating yourself and very likely, having a great time doing it. Now, so that you'll be better able organize your material, always do the following:

- ❖ Date photographs or notes. You may think you'll remember exactly when you saw a specific home or room or office, but you may not.

- ❖ Record the addresses! This sounds elementary, but if you want to go back later to see one of the interiors again, you may not remember where you saw it.

- ❖ Jot down the mood of the room or home.

- ❖ Jot down any special design ideas that appeal to you; that trigger your interest, or seem especially attractive to you.

NOTE: Always assume that you'll forget a detail you've seen and will later want to remember.

Once you have a list of professional interior designers referred to you and/or whose work you admire, it's time for you to meet with them. It's not uncommon to talk with two or three or even four designers before you make your decision. Remember that each of you is interviewing the other.

Before you meet with an interior designer, take stock of your practical as well as your design requirements. Have ready a list of your special needs so that as you talk with the designer, you're covering all bases. Do you want to update your living room? Do you want the interiors of your entire home designed and furnished? Have you recently bought new electronic equipment, such as a large TV screen, computer, or the components of a music system that needs to be integrated into your home?

Be open-minded. Be prepared to listen. After all, ideas are the stock and trade of designers.

Take notes! Again, this sounds so obvious, but it isn't. It's easier than you now think, to become so engrossed in a conversation that you forget precisely what the designer said. You'll be amazed at how certain details, which you thought were important at the time, have escaped you later.

Do Not Be Intimidated

So that your home will reflect you, your interior designer may ask for your input throughout your entire project. Your completed home must express who you are. At all times it's important to remember that you can agree to disagree—and still remain friends. Honesty is essential.

Share information about yourself, your family, and your colors. If your family goes in every direction every night and having dinner together is a sometime event, the designer should know that. If you enjoy formal entertaining, the designer needs to know that as well. Although budget is very important it's also important to remember that the major reason you're engaging the services of an interior designer, is because you want a well designed home, and at this time design is be your primary concern.

And it is necessary to be absolutely straightforward with your designer about your budget restrictions. As you work together you'll find that various design concepts can be translated into a variety of dollar costs. Sometimes, there will be ways you'll be able to achieve the look you want at a lower cost. Your designer will know if and how this can be done. Again, keep your mind open to all ideas presented to you.

When you're interviewing a designer, ask how he or she would feel if you disagree with a color scheme, fabric, or furnishing selection. You'll be able to tell a lot about the interior designer's attitude when you listen carefully to the responses to your questions. The answers you receive, and the attitude of the designer when she is responding to you, will give you a good understanding of whether or not both of you can work together.

What About Color?

Although recently more magazines have been featuring interiors where color is used, many designers are not accustomed to using color in important ways in home interiors. They still rely on throw pillows and art hanging on the walls for real color. However, now that you know the colors you want to live with, it's very important that you tell the designer that having color in your home is your focus now.

It's not uncommon to be told by the designer who feels uncertain with real color and prefers to use "neutral colors"—a euphemism for beige, browns, and off-white (yet another euphemism for white) that 'You'll grow tired of that color.' 'That combination is too busy.' Rather than give in, give this designer up. She/he is not for you.

You want to work with someone who will enthusiastically embrace colors and use them so skillfully that whenever you even think of you're home, you find yourself smiling with delight.

However, if you love grey and beige, by all means, use them. Grey and beige are very good colors, as are all colors. However, don't limit yourself to an *all*-neutral scheme relieved by colored throw pillows, simply because you're being pressured by a well-meaning designer. Always remember that *you are the only person who can decide which colors are right for you.*

What About Trendy?

The cost of furniture today is too high to spend your money on anything that will in ten years look like yesterday's furniture. Be careful about agreeing to trendy furnishings in your home should you feel that the cost of these items puts them in the category of 'expensive.' Trendy furnishings will definitely date a room. Use discretion when choosing so-called 'fashionable' furnishings and major accessories. Rarely do any of these pieces turn out to be timeless classics. The great majority will be relegated to the wasteland of outmoded fad. Yet, while your budget might survive a fling with a piece of furniture you like now, and twenty years from now it will look like you purchased it during the first part of the 21st century, think hard before taking a chance on a several thousand dollar trendy sofa. Look for quality workmanship, fine fabrics, beautiful woods, comfort and *timeless style*. Like good people, fine furnishings 'wear well.' Stay with classic, well designed, timeless styles for your major pieces.

What About Deadlines?

Tell your designer exactly when you would need to have your project completed. Is there an important deadline you would like to meet, such as a family wedding? At the beginning of your relationship let the designer in on any possible time restrictions so that he or she can determine whether the time frame for completion is realistic.

Who Makes The Final Decisions?

Expect your designer to ask whether you're a person who makes quick, firm decisions or whether you need a long time to make up your mind. Do you often find yourself lying awake at night with what some people suffer from—buyer's remorse? Designers need to feel comfortable with clients before agreeing to work with them, and these kind of practical, basic questions should be answered early in a designer-client relationship.

There are designers who can and do cope with clients whose uncertainty after having made their decisions, deeply concern them. It's best and wise to candidly tell the interior designer what to expect from you if you're both to work well together. If you often worry about decisions you've made, reveal this—it's how you are. She'll respect you for telling her and because she's prepared, she'll be able to work through it with you. I have a client who *always worries about everything*. She knows it—I know it—and we both work her through it. She's been my client for 20 years and I love her in spite of her frailty, and for her honesty about it. I always remember that I, too, have a few frailties.

It's up to you to decide how closely you want to stay involved in the details of your project and if you prefer to receive frequent updates on the status of the carpeting, paint, wallpaper, window treatment, and furnishings. If, however, you have a time-consuming, high-pressure career, you may be delighted to turn all the nitty-gritty design details over to your interior designer and feel assured that she's taking care of providing you with the beautiful home you're expecting it to be.

As long as each of you knows where the other stands, neither stance should pose a problem. Again, always be completely honest with your designer with regard to your needs, your preferences, and your budget.

You will usually find that if you take time to do some groundwork before deciding to use a particular designer your relationship will be smooth and harmonious. Neither of you will experience unhappy surprises.

You and your interior designer will be able to work together on a satisfying professional and personal level designing your home so that it reflects your unique personality. When it comes to discovering the real you, there is no place like home to begin!

Chapter Eleven
So Now...Color Your Life!

*Oscar Wilde said, "Color speaks to the
soul in a thousand different ways."*

It's an understatement to say that color is far and away more important than we
know. When life puts us into overwhelm, this natural element we all thrive with,
and rarely think of as vital to our mental health, is too often overlooked as a key
element to restore our spirits.

However, this is not to say that living with the colors we love will solve our
problems. But color does have an instant soothing effect upon us, and its gentle
and life affirming serenity imbues us with the feeling and awareness that these
now difficult times will pass; that our lives are changing for the better. Color
speaks to us in a language all its own.

We know that our homes are much more to us than shelter and where we
eat and sleep. Our homes are where our hearts are and more often than we realize,
how we think of ourselves has a lot to do with how we feel about our homes.

We all carry with us remnants of our childhood—both good and bad. Also,
we know that when a time of life ends, very often we remain connected to it. Our
memories of that period we lived through is the glue that keeps us cleaved to our
past. And because we have a natural relationship to color, we're often emotionally
affected by colors that were present during certain pivotal times of our lives.

We know that we can trust our color memory because it's a powerful emotional palette. Color and emotion are so completely intertwined that we can
recall certain situations, good and bad, that happened many years ago—in color.

When we see an unbelievably beautiful, impossible to describe sunset, or
enjoy the exquisitely gorgeous colors of a garden in bloom, we're realizing the joy
of our spiritual connection to color. And we're experiencing the pleasure of life in
living color.

This is the final chapter of *Color Your Life.* By now you've looked around your home and mentally begun to redecorate. This time you feel certain that your home will look like you.

I'm sure that it will. What will make the difference? Color will make the difference. Color, the most inexpensive, most available and natural element on the planet will transform your home from ordinary to delightful. And the easiest, most affordable way to make it happen is with paint.

Use paint as you would a condiment to your food. Paint is as mustard is to a frankfurter, as extra virgin olive oil is to a delicious salad dressing, as cabbage is to corned beef. It's that basic. Paint in beautiful colors is the always-reliable element that will enhance your home. Paint is the Great Enhancer for every room in your home.

This time, as you begin to design a room in your home, you'll feel confident that you're using colors you love. You'll trust your color memory, that powerful emotional palette you carry in your heart. You understand that color and emotion are so completely entwined that we can instantly recall a vivid memory in living color—as though it were happening today.

By unlocking your color memory, you've discovered a tool that will allow you to design your home with your heart—instead of with your head. And allowing your heart to be part of the decisions you make for your home will account for the special warmth your home feels and looks to you, and to those who spend any time in it.

You've taken the Supermarket Test, so you know your true colors. You've checked your wardrobe and learned more about the colors you love. Through the Sleep Test, even your subconscious has gotten into the act.

You've learned that all colors go together naturally—the Color Bars have proven this to you. You've become familiar with the Color Bars, and know that all the colors are matched—coordinated to each other so that you will never make a color mistake when using them.

You've awakened to the truth that you can lift a room from the ordinary to outstanding, by adding color in important ways to the room, and it will instantly express your personality.

All that's left now is for you to lose the final inhibitions and let your instincts and your spirit soar.

Of course, not everyone can soar immediately. No matter how strong our intentions, many of us begin new projects with a tentative urge rather than with an all-out commitment. If this describes you, you may prefer to begin by using color in moderation.

To do this, use only one of your colors—a color you found when you took the Supermarket Test, to which you joyfully responded. Use this color on only two walls in a room painted this color, or a lounge chair upholstered in your color. As you feel comfortable with that color, you'll find that your confidence level will increase and soon you'll be planning colors in every room of your house. It's then that you'll be ready to soar!

Given time, you'll learn to trust and follow your natural instincts. You'll suddenly know that without any doubt you can live with beautiful color in your home. One day you may say, as a client told me, "My house is going to look like me. I'm excited beyond any way I can express. When I took the Supermarket Test and saw the gorgeous eggplant I'd chosen, and the carrot against it, I became a believer and I'm convinced that I need to have these colors in my home." That's what color confidence does for you.

Writing this book and taking my message on the road through television and radio, has been an ongoing joy for me. I've experienced so many memorable moments. I recall a radio talk show in Florida when an eighty-year-old man phoned in to tell me, "At last, somebody understands that regardless of how old we are, we all want our bedrooms to be sensuous."

And the night the CNN telephone lines in Atlanta were jammed with callers—at 2:00 a.m.—to tell me of their color memories, and how those memories affected their lives many years later. Wherever I've traveled, I've found that people are fascinated to find that they can follow their own natural color instincts with great success in their environments.

This is what I wish for you…that designing your home and using the colors God has given you leaves you feeling deeply fulfilled. And that you realize the joy of living with wonderful, memorable, life-affirming color that will enhance your life so that your spirit will soar.

To Note What You Want to Remember

Glossary of Decorative Terms

Acrylic Backed Fabric
A fabric to which an acrylic spray is applied professionally to give it extra strength so it may be used for upholstery. This differs from paper backed fabric, to which a paper finish is applied so it can be used as wall covering.

Amethyst (color)
A variable color averaging moderate purple to graying reddish purple.

Antique
Furniture, porcelain, glass, a painting, or any article which according to United States Law is at least 100 years old.

Arc Lamp
A popular style during the Seventies, featuring a light suspended from a large, curved stem. The base of the lamp is usually four to six feet below the light.

Bauhaus
A school of art and architecture founded at Weimar, Germany (1919), and headed by Walter Gropius. It stressed respect for materials and design techniques.

Bolster/Bolstered
A long, narrow pillow or cushion. To support or prop up with such a pillow.

Broadloom
Carpet woven on a wide loom, up to eighteen feet in width, often in a solid color.

Bronze Mirror
Mirror with a deep brownish tinge. Bronze mirrors add drama to a room; they are also flattering.

Canopy
A cloth covering suspended over a bed. Canopies add romance, importance, even mystery to a bedroom.

Cape Cod cottage
A compact one- or one-and-a-half story rectangular house usually with a steep gabled roof and a central chimney. Named for such homes in Cape Cod, Massachusetts.

Chenille
A woven fabric that has a velvety feel and a luxurious weight. Chenille is often used in living and family rooms for upholstering sofas, lounge chairs and seating units. Chenille is known to be a durable fabric and will take a lot of wear.

Chintz
A printed and glazed cotton fabric, often of bright colors.

Country French (style)
A charming architectural and interior design style, used in the provinces of France during the 17th and 18th centuries. Country French gives a naive and spontaneous effect.

Couture
The business of designing, making, and selling fashionable custom-made women's clothing.

Damask
A firm, lustrous fabric of linen, cotton, silk, or rayon, woven with flat, elegant patterns in a satin weave on plain-woven background.

Document Prints
Usually cotton fabric, with a very small floral pattern in one to three colors. The pattern is repeated frequently, one-quarter to one-half inch apart. Use this versatile print with absolute confidence because it lends itself to almost anything imaginable—from kitchen curtains to important upholstered pieces.

Faille
A slightly ribbed, woven fabric of cotton, silk, or rayon.

Flat Paint
Paint that does not have a sheen.

Gauze
A thin, transparent fabric with a loose open weave, often used for curtains.

Greige	A term that is used to describe a gray-beige color. The term greige is also used to describe the color of textiles in an unbleached, undyed state as taken from the loom.
Grosgrain	A heavy silk or rayon fabric with narrow horizontal ribs, most often used for ribbon.
Hue	The true color, itself. Many tones of the same hue are possible.
Lacquer	A glossy, often resinous material, used as a surface covering, applied in coats. Lacquer-work was one of the earliest industrial arts of the Orient. It is used today in furniture from India and China.
Moiré	Cloth, usually silk, that has a watered or wavy pattern.
Monochromatic	Having only one color or hue.
Nappy Velvet	A term that describes the quality of velvet, a fabric with a thick, short pile.
Panne Velvet	Velvet that has an especially shiny or lustrous surface.
Parquet	A floor of parquetry; that is, wood, often of contrasting colors, worked into an inlaid mosaic.
Pongee	A thin, soft fabric woven from silk, with a knotty weave. It is now available in synthetic fibers. Pongee has an interesting texture and is very durable. Use for draw curtains or where a flowing quality is desired in a room.
Pouf/Poufed	A bouffant or fluffy part of a garment or accessory. To puff up or make fluffy.
Ranch House(style)	A rectangular, one-story house, usually with a low-pitched roof and open plan.
Ready-made	Already made, prepared, or available, usually referring to garments. Many lovely and appropriate decorative accessories for the home come ready-made as well.

Roman shades	Flat, fabric shades that draw up with cords sewn to the back. Do not confuse these with the Austrian shade, which is soft and drapey, or you will be disappointed in the finished effect.
Scored Concrete	Concrete that is etched when it is freshly laid and still damp to give it the appearance of tile. This is a good design treatment, effective both inside and outside a home.
Semi-etagere	A small or short version of a full-length etagere—a piece of furniture with open shelves for ornaments. This requires frequent dusting.
Shade	A tone produced by adding black, grey, white, or some other color to a main color. The easiest way to imagine a shade is to think of it as the darker gradation of a color. No matter which shade *you* select, your *mother* would probably choose a different one.
Shantung	A heavy fabric, made of silk, with a rough, nubby surface.
Shirr	Fabric gathered on a rod for a window treatment. Shirred fabric is often used to created dust ruffles for the lower portion of the bed.
Terra Cotta Tile	A flooring tile made from hard, semifired, waterproof ceramic clay. Usually a brownish orange color.
Louis Comfort Tiffany	American artist and designer (1848-1933). Known for the iridescent colors and natural forms of his stained glass vases, lamps, and windows.
Tint	A gradation of color made by adding white. A pale or delicate variation of a color.
Tone	The gradations of a color from its palest to its darkest.
Tone-On-Tone	The same tone woven into a fabric of the same color. The effect of two tones creates a different texture on the fabric.

Valance   An ornamental drapery hung across a topo edge, as of a bed, table, or canopy. Or, a short drapery, decorative board, or metal strip mounted across the top of a window to conceal structural fixtures.

Voile   A fine, soft, sheer fabric of cotton, rayon, silk or wool used for making curtains or dresses. Used with abandon, this fabric adds romance to a room.

Wedgwood   A type of pottery made originally by Josiah Wedgwood (1730–1795). "Wedgwood blue" is named for Wedgwood jasper ware, famous for its rich blue color, the background for white cameo-like figures.

Wrap/Wrapped   A design treatment which is to envelop or sheath a room floor to ceiling entirely in fabric, and often also on the ceiling, to create maximum color and/or pattern impact.

To Note What You Want to Remember

Index